THE ART OF
AUBREY BEARDSLEY

THE ART OF
AUBREY BEARDSLEY

CATHERINE SLESSOR

SILVERDALE BOOKS

A QUANTUM BOOK

This edition published by Silverdale Books,
an imprint of Bookmart Ltd., in 2004

Bookmart Ltd.
Blaby Road
Wigston
Leicester
LE18 4SE

This edition printed 2004

ISBN 1-84509-089-6

QUMBDY

Printed in Singapore by
Star Standard Industries (Pte) Ltd.

CONTENTS

INTRODUCTION

AUBREY BEARDSLEY lived in an age when design and the 'applied' arts – illustration, graphics, ceramics and jewellery, for example – were undergoing a significant transformation. Up to the middle of the 19th century, applied arts were generally considered inferior to the 'fine' arts of painting and sculpture, but critical attitudes were destined to change. An important early milestone in this cultural renaissance was the 1861 formation by William Morris of his own design firm, Morris, Marshall, Faulkner & Co. Their prospectus stated unequivocally that 'the growth of decorative art in this country [England] has now reached a point at which it seems desirable that artists of reputation should devote their time to it.'

This helped to establish the idea that 'proper' artists could now legitimately practice the arts of design, and laid the groundwork for what eventually became known as the Arts and Crafts Movement.

By the 1890s the arts of design had become increasingly dominant in England, causing critic and designer Gleeson White to write in *The Studio* magazine:

'Today is essentially a time when mean things are done so finely, that future ages may refer to it as a period when the minor arts attracted the genius and energy now – from modesty or timidity – directed from heroic enterprises.'

Taken from an article published in 1893, this statement provides a clue to understanding Beardlsey's art in the medium of illustration. The fact that Beardsley's dazzling reputation, both in his own time and over the past hundred years, is based on mechanical reproductions of his work is one of the most astonishing in the history of art. Unlike a painting in a gallery, it is only between the covers of a book that the essence of Beardsley's art can be fully appreciated.

From the beginning, Beardsley's natural and most powerful means of expression was through drawing. This vision led him to develop a graphic style in which line predominated over tone.

RIGHT

A full page illustration from *Le Morte d'Arthur*, Beardsley's first major commission. The highly stylized floral border and the precise juxtaposition of flat planes of black and white demonstrate at this early stage in his career an exceptional talent at work

HOW LA BEALE
ISOVD WROTE TO
SIR TRISTRAM

This proved well suited to the processes of photo-mechanical reproduction which were developed and refined during the latter half of the 19th century. The technique of line block in particular enabled Beardsley's work to be reproduced with a high degree of accuracy.

Allied to low cost and the potential of mass production, Beardsley managed to reach an unprecedentedly wide audience for a major artist. He thus occupies an important place in the 'democratization' of art which occurred throughout the 19th century, starting gradually with the growth of public art galleries and exhibitions, and finally accelerated by the advent of photo-mechanical methods of reproduction.

At the time Beardsley's art undoubtedly created a tremendous stir. His success was more of a *succès de scandale* than a measure of his skill, and his fame constantly bordered on notoriety. Shock at the overtly erotic nature of his subject matter was further increased by the originality of his graphic style. Contemporary public response to his work is perhaps best summed up by the now-famous comments from *The Westminster Gazette* describing Beardsley's contribution to the first issue of *The Yellow Book*. 'We do not know of anything that would meet the case except a short Act of Parliament to make this kind of thing illegal.'

Henceforth Beardsley was labelled as a 'Decadent'. In the context of the art and literature of the late 19th century, Decadence was merely an extreme form of Romanticism, a movement which attempted to express an artistic response to the cultural changes wrought by the Industrial Revolution. As European society became increasingly dominated by the materialistic demands of wealth creation, artistic and spiritual life came under increasing pressure to conform within the strict social and moral conventions established by the new ruling bourgeoisie. The primary concern of Decadent artists was to depict those aspects of society and human behaviour that were either repressed or ignored.

In this respect, they were part of the influential Realist movement which was founded in the mid-19th century by the painter Gustave Courbet and the writer Emile Zola. The crucial difference between the two was that whereas the Realists endowed their art with the grit and rawness of everyday life, the Decadent approach aimed to make their subject matter as exquisite as possible. They tended to avoid dealing with working-class or peasant life, and instead concentrated their attentions on the depiction of sexuality, another great area of Victorian repression.

Sexuality is one of the principal themes of all great art, and for Decadent artists such as Beardsley it offered immense scope for

RIGHT
The cover for the first issue of *The Studio* magazine which contained a number of Beardsley's early drawings and an appraisal of his work by the distinguished critic Joseph Pennell who wrote: 'Beardsley is an artist whose work is quite remarkable in its execution as it is in its invention, a very rare combination.'

lyrical treatment. It was also regarded as the key to a world of warmth, pleasure and fantasy – a complete antithesis to the harsh, ugly realities of the Victorian Age. But although there is a strong element of escapism among the Decadents their art was not purely hedonistic and sensuous, like that of their Impressionist contemporaries. Their work, as embodied by Beardsley, is always tinged with an awareness of mortality, tragedy, and the bittersweet essence of human vanity.

RIGHT
An illustration for *The Mask of the Red Death* by Edgar Allan Poe. The drawing is populated by a strange assortment of bizarre characters and this fascination with human oddity was to become a hallmark of Beardsley's illustrative style.

CHAPTER ONE

THE EARLY YEARS ... BRIGHTON, LONDON, PARIS

AUBREY VINCENT BEARDSLEY was born in the fashionable town of Brighton on the south coast of England on August 21, 1872. His mother, Ellen Agnus Beardsley, nèe Pitt, came from a well-heeled middle-class family and was something of a local charmer. There is considerable speculation among art historians that Beardsley's famous drawing of the actress Mrs Patrick Campbell is in fact an idealized image of Ellen Beardsley, since it bears so little relation to its ostensible subject. One of the dominant influences on his life and career, Beardsley's mother remained, despite his notorious artistic and personal reputation, resolutely loyal and unshockable to the last.

His father, Vincent Beardsley, had married Ellen Pitt in 1870, largely on the strength of her inheritance, which unfortunately proved insufficient to sustain the marriage. As a result, the family was dogged by poverty from around the time of Aubrey's birth, and Beardsley himself was to remain poignantly conscious of the importance of money – or rather the lack of it – for most of his life.

Both Beardsley and his elder sister Mabel, born in 1871, were brought up largely by their mother, since their father was afflicted with tuberculosis. His mother became the economic mainstay of the household, working as a governess and music teacher. Strangely enough, Beardsley's parents never had a permanent home in Brighton, and the children were brought up in the house of their maternal grandfather, a retired surgeon major. The slightly faded, genteel atmosphere of Brighton and its architecture clearly had a profound effect on Beardsley's pictorial imagination, and several of his drawings echo the crazy rococo-chinoiserie of the Brighton Pavilion, as well as the regimented grandeur of the sweeping Regency terraces.

Beardsley's early education began at home, with a vengeance. Ellen Beardsley insisted on training her children musically, playing to them a repertoire of half a dozen pieces every evening and

RIGHT
An illustration by the English artist Kate Greenaway whose work played an important part in the revival of book design and illustration during the Arts and Crafts Movement of the mid-nineteenth century.

RIGHT
Although Beardsley was influenced by the technique of artists such as Kate Greenaway, his own drawings were instilled with a sensual potency, epitomized by this frontispiece for 'An Evil Motherhood'.

overseeing their choice of reading in a similar fashion. By the time Beardsley went to boarding school in 1879, he was something of a musical prodigy and exceptionally literate for his age.

Hamilton Lodge, Hurstpierpoint, near Brighton on the South Downs, was chosen for its supposedly healthful situation, since the young Beardsley had already begun to exhibit the symptoms of the tuberculosis, inherited from his father, which was to kill him 19 years later. Ellen Beardsley was well aware that Aubrey was a weak, fragile child – 'like a delicate piece of Dresden china'. At Hamilton Lodge, Beardsley began to compose poetry and to draw regularly, as well as pursuing his musical studies.

In the autumn of 1881 Ellen Beardsley decided to move to Epsom for the sake of her son's health, and the family remained there for two years. During this period, Beardsley, then aged 10, received his first paid commission for drawings, from Lady Henrietta Pelham, a friend of the family. The drawings were, in effect,

copies made from books written and illustrated by the English artist Kate Greenaway, whose work occupied an important place in the revival of book design and illustration that was taking place under the auspices of the Arts & Crafts movement. Greenaway's books were printed in colour from woodblocks, a technique developed by the influential designer and illustrator Walter Crane in 1865. Stylistically, the illustrations are unusually flat, oversimplified and decorative, but these qualities were to form the basis of Beardsley's mature technique.

Not long after the young prodigy's first brush with a patroness of the arts, the Beardsley family moved to London. Encouraged as always by their mother, both Aubrey and Mabel became extensively involved in giving drawing-room recitals and concerts, at receptions held by her friends and patrons.

But continuing financial difficulties forced a return to Brighton in the summer of 1884, where Aubrey, Mabel and their mother

went to live with a comfortably well-off relative, Sarah Pitt. It was she who undertook to pay Beardsley's fees to Brighton Grammar School where he completed his formal education. He brought with him a formidable array of accomplishments – a little French, a taste and aptitude for music, literature and art, coupled with a will of iron and a strange, eccentric arrogance.

His housemaster at Brighton Grammar was Arthur King, a remarkable man who recognized Beardsley's talent, and collected his drawings for publication in the school magazine. King was also passionately fond of the theatre, and organized several theatricals at the school in which the young Beardsley played an active part. This marked the beginning of a deep and significant attachment to the theatre in all its forms. Throughout his life the theatre was a major source of inspiration and provided a constant frame of reference for Beardsley's work. It is no surprise, therefore, to discover that his first notable collection of illustrations was for the programme of a comic opera, *The Pay of the Pied Piper*, staged by Brighton Grammar School at the end of 1888, shortly after Beardsley had left school. By that time the family

LEFT
An illustration for *Goldilocks and the Three Bears* by Walter Crane, another formative influence on Beardsley.

LEFT
King Cophetua and the Beggar Maid by Edward Burne-Jones. Beardsley was attracted to Burne-Jones's dreamy, romantic paintings, and an encounter with the artist at his studio in 1891 finally convinced Beardsley that his future lay in art.

RIGHT
A sketch of the painter Frederick Brown, under whose tutelage Beardsley spent a year at the Westminster School of Art from 1891–92. Remarkably this was the only formal artistic training he ever undertook.

RIGHT
The famous 'Peacock Room' decorated by the American artist James McNeill Whistler. The sweeping, linear, Japanese style murals are one of the earliest examples of Art Nouveau interior design. Whistler's own painting, *La Princesse du Pays au Porcelaine* hangs over the fireplace. Beardsley was enthralled by this rich, sensual environment.

were once again in London, living in Pimlico, where Mabel and Aubrey founded their own amateur theatre, The Cambridge Theatre of Varieties. The name derived from the family home at 32, Cambridge Street.

THOUGHT, POETRY AND IMAGINATION

But the real world proved less than inspiring. At the age of 16, Beardsley had little alternative but to submit to the drudgery of employment as a clerk – first temporarily in the Clerkenwell District Surveyor's office, and then from January 1889 in a permanent post with the Guardian Life Assurance Company in the City of London. But he continued to pursue more stimulating distractions such as books and the theatre, as a letter written to his ex-housemaster Arthur King clearly shows: 'I went to Macbeth last week. I was delighted with it . . . I have been "in business" since New Year's Day. I don't exactly dislike it, but am not as yet frantically attached. My work is, however, not hard.'

Nonetheless, soon after he had started work in London Beardsley began to experience the shocks and exhaustion of consumptive attacks. Tuberculosis, inherited from his father, had been diagnosed in 1879, and this first serious attack kept

Beardsley away from his job for an entire year. During this time he more or less deliberately gave up drawing, and, encouraged by the publication of one of his short stories, made a concerted effort to embark upon a literary career.

But in the spring of 1891 his health gradually improved, and he returned to his work in the insurance office and, more importantly, to his drawing. He subsequently wrote to Arthur King: '. . . I don't think I put pencil to paper for a good year. In vain I tried to crush it out of me, but that drawing faculty would come uppermost. So I submit to the inevitable.'

The event which led Beardsley to finally acknowledge the fact that his future lay in art as opposed to literature was a visit he made with his sister to the studio of Edward Burne-Jones in the summer of 1891. Burne-Jones was then in the final years of his life – he died in 1898 – but in his day was one of the most prominent English artists, as well as an influential designer and illustrator. He was a key figure in the Arts & Crafts movement, being one of the founder members of the firm of William Morris and Company in 1861, and produced several tapestry and stained glass designs for the company. Beardsley was strongly drawn to Burne-Jones's dreamy, romantic paintings, and was eager to

RIGHT

The romantic influence of Burne-Jones is evident in much of Beardsley's early work. This drawing entitled *Hamlet following the Ghost of his Father* depicts Hamlet as a sallow emaciated youth trapped in a menacing forest. Both the figure and the setting owe a clear stylistic debt to Burne-Jones.

meet the artist and see more of his work. During their first meeting at Burne-Jones's studio, Beardsley asked the painter to give his opinion on a portfolio of drawings he had with him.

As Beardsley recalls, Burne-Jones's response was unequivocal: 'All are full of thought, poetry and imagination. Nature has given you every gift which is necessary to become a great artist. I seldom or never advise anyone to take up art as a profession, but in your case I can do nothing else.'

Burne-Jones promised to find Beardsley a suitable art school, and after considering several possibilities, Beardsley embarked upon a course of night classes at the Westminster School of Art under the direction of the English Impressionist painter Frederick Brown. He continued to attend classes for just over a year, from 1881 to 1882, and remarkably, this was the only formal artistic training he ever undertook.

Shortly before his visit to Burne-Jones, Beardsley had received another decisive stimulus. He was invited to the house of Frederick Leyland, a wealthy patron of the arts, where he saw a large collection of paintings by Burne-Jones and the English pre-Raphaelite painter Dante Gabriel Rossetti, Burne-Jones's teacher and friend. Rossetti's subjects were drawn from work by the Italian poet Dante and a medieval dream world, which charged his paintings with a disturbing, romantic intensity. Beardsley described them as 'glorious'.

He also saw the famous 'Peacock Room', Leyland's dining room, which had been decorated to stunning effect by the American artist James McNeill Whistler, with murals of sweeping, linear, Japanese style peacocks in blue, silver and gold. Whistler had also hung in the room a large painting, *La Princesse du Pays de Porcelaine*, which Beardsley described in a letter to a friend: 'The figure is very beautiful and gorgeously painted, the colour being principally old gold.'

THE CREATION OF A STYLE

The combined effect of Burne-Jones, Whistler and Frederick Brown's evening classes produced a rapid acceleration of Beardsley's artistic development in late 1891 and early 1892. In the space of a mere six months the basis of his mature style was evolved. At the start of this period the influence of Burne-Jones still predominates, as studies of his drawings executed at the time clearly reveal. One in particular, *Hamlet following the Ghost of his Father*, shows a distinct stylistic debt to Burne-Jones, as Hamlet, depicted as an emaciated youth, gropes his way gingerly through a menacing and seemingly impenetrable forest. It is tempting to connect this image with Beardsley's famous description of himself, written just before he executed the drawing, as 'eighteen years old, with a vile constitution, a sallow face and sunken eyes, long red hair, a shuffling gait and a stoop'.

Other drawings of late 1891 and early 1892 display the influence of the Italian Renaissance painter Mantegna, and the English designer and illustrator Walter Crane. But it was in the spring of 1892, following yet another bout of illness which prevented him from drawing, that Beardsley began a series of remarkable drawings which were to prove a significant turning point in his career. In these works, the effects of Japanese art and Whistler's modernism suddenly manifest themselves in a style which Beardsley later described as 'an entirely new method of drawing and composition, suggestive of Japan, but not really Japanesque'.

This technique was characterized by the presence of arabesques and areas of black ink given texture by slight abrasions, artfully juxtaposed or dis-balanced in order to dramatize the subject of the drawing without lifting it from an almost geometric purity of line. This was, in effect, Beardsley's tribute to the Japanese printmakers of the 18th and 19th centuries. Following the reopening of trade with Japan in the 1850s, Japanese woodblock prints began to flood into Europe. These stylized, decorative non-naturalistic works presented European artists with a new set of pictorial conventions governing the representation of the real world.

At last Beardsley had discovered a personal style in which his own unique vision of the world sprang fully into being, endowed with a compulsive quality which was to become his hallmark. His choice of subject matter was also innovative, combining highly stylized human forms with lavish and exotic decoration. He himself wrote that 'the subjects were quite mad and a little indecent. Strange hermaphrodite creatures wandering about in Pierrot costumes or modern dress, quite a new world of my own creation.'

A notable early example is *The Birthday of Madame Cigale*, which features a procession of astonishingly bizarre visitors bearing gifts for the half-naked Madame Cigale, a severe, aristocratic-looking courtesan. This drawing already displays the technical skill of which Beardsley boasted; 'In certain points of technique I achieved something like perfection at once.'

With it emerges one of the most significant characteristics of Beardsley's art – his ability to express even the most bizarre fantasies in forms of great purity. This is eloquently summarized by Beardsley's description of his 'new' drawings as 'extremely

RIGHT
These two drawings were executed while Beardsley was working as a clerk in an insurance office. The self-portrait parodies his famous description of himself written in 1890 – 'I am now eighteen years old, with a vile constitution, a sallow face and sunken eyes, long red hair, a shuffling gait and a stoop.' The other drawing depicts Beardsley at his desk in the insurance office, a job he loathed. This symbolic self-portrait suggests that his creative energies are being sapped by a tedious daily routine but it is also one of the earliest examples of a new type of drawing style in which forms are defined by scarcely more than a single outline to create an effect of austere beauty.

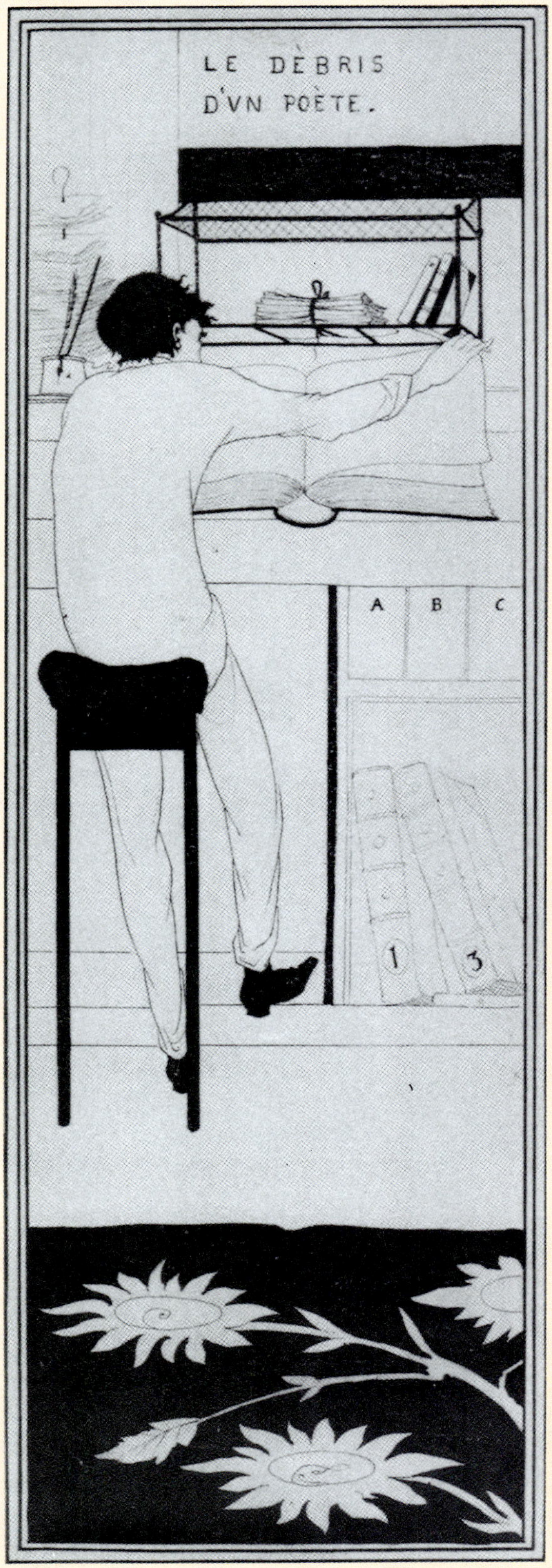
LE DÈBRIS
D'VN POÈTE.
A B C
1 3

ABOVE

The Birthday of Madame Cigale combines highly stylised human forms with lavish and exotic decoration. At the time Beardsley wrote: 'The subjects were quite mad and a little indecent. Strange hermaphrodite creatures wandering about in pierrot costumes or modern dress, quite a new world of my own creation.'

fantastic in conception, but perfectly severe in execution'.

Other drawings in the same series, completed at a later date, match the severity of execution with a new compositional restraint, which eliminates the abundance of decorative detail present in *Madame Cigale*.

One drawing in particular, *Le Débris d'un Poete* is significant for the way in which Beardsley displays for the first time his ability to compose a drawing in a 'musical' way, with 'notes' of solid black placed in a finely judged relationship to each other, and balanced against large areas of white.

Forms are defined by scarcely more than a single outline, to create an effect of austere beauty. But this restraint does not diminish the expressive power of the image, which could as easily be a monk, or an alchemist at work, as the clerk the drawing purports to represent.

The title translates somewhat enigmatically as *The Wreck of a Poet*, a phrase lifted from the French novel *Madame Bovary* by Gustave Flaubert, which states that in many a notary there is the *débris* of a poet. Like his earlier drawing of Hamlet, this can be seen as a symbolic self-portrait, showing Beardsley at his desk in a job he found increasingly oppressive. By representing himself as a mere penpusher, stuck in an office, he suggests that his creative energies are being sapped by both disease and a tedious daily routine. In his earliest drawings in the 'Japonesque' manner Beardsley lightened the areas of black ink by scratching and rubbing the dried surfaces.

In this drawing Beardsley established a basic vocabulary of style and technique, with carefully balanced masses of pure black and white, which characterized his best work throughout his career. But he also continued to use the fantastic, highly-wrought style of *Madame Cigale* with its proliferation of tendril-like fine lines and decorative flourishes. Indeed, elaborate composition and dense, Rococo-like linework remained an essential element of Beardsley's art, particularly in the expression of fantastic or highly imaginative themes.

In June 1892 Beardsley used his annual holiday to visit Paris for the first time. He took with him a portfolio of new drawings, hoping to stimulate a reaction to his work from both artists and critics in the city that was the undisputed centre of modern art. Judging from his letters, the trip was an unqualified success. He was energetically received by the president of the Salon des Beaux Arts, Pierre Puvis de Chavannes, who introduced him to other artists as *un jeune artist Anglais qui fait des choses étonnant* (a young English artist who does astonishing things).

Puvis de Chavannes occupied the most powerful position in French art – the equivalent to the president of The Royal Academy in England – but he was also well respected by the avant-garde fraternity. His opinion, therefore, carried a particular weight with Beardsley, but the signs are that other French artists also reacted to his work with surprise and enthusiasm. Beardsley was greatly encouraged by all this favourable attention. 'I was not a little pleased, I can tell you, with my success,' he wrote.

Fired by the acclaim, he returned to London later that summer.

CHAPTER TWO
THE IMPORTANT EARLY COMMISSIONS LE MORTE D'ARTHUR & SALOME

AUBREY BEARDSLEY'S considerable success in Paris was followed almost immediately by success of a more tangible kind in London. The young artist had become friendly with Frederick Evans, a bookseller, in whose shop in Cheapside Beardsley used to browse during his lunch hours. Evans was also an accomplished photographer who, in 1895, took the most memorable of all of the Beardsley portraits. Around the autumn of 1892, Evans introduced Beardsley to the publisher J M Dent, who at that time was looking for an artist to illustrate the medieval English version of the legend of King Arthur, *Le Morte d'Arthur,* written by Sir Thomas Malory and first published by William Caxton in 1485.

Dent intended that his edition of *Le Morte d'Arthur* should be in the rich, ornate medieval style inspired originally by Caxton, but which had come to characterize the illustrated and decorated books produced by William Morris at his Kelmscott Press, founded in 1889. True to the principles of the Arts & Crafts movement, Kelmscott books were hand-printed in strictly limited editions, and usually illustrated by Edward Burne-Jones, with decorations by Morris. Both illustrations and decorations were printed using laboriously hand-cut wooden blocks.

Dent had no time for this painstaking method of production. He was aiming to achieve the same effect more cheaply, reaching a wider audience, by taking advantage of new photographic methods of reproduction. At that first encounter with Beardsley, Dent examined a selection of Beardsley's work and then, as a test, asked him to provide a sample illustration of a theme in *Le Morte d'Arthur*. Beardsley quickly responded by producing *The Achieving of the Sangreal*, which used a more conventional technique of line and wash, adapted to the medieval subject matter. When presented with this drawing, Dent immediately concluded a verbal agreement with Beardsley, engaging him to illustrate the whole of *Le Morte d'Arthur* in two volumes, which were to be issued to subscribers in a series of monthly parts. The

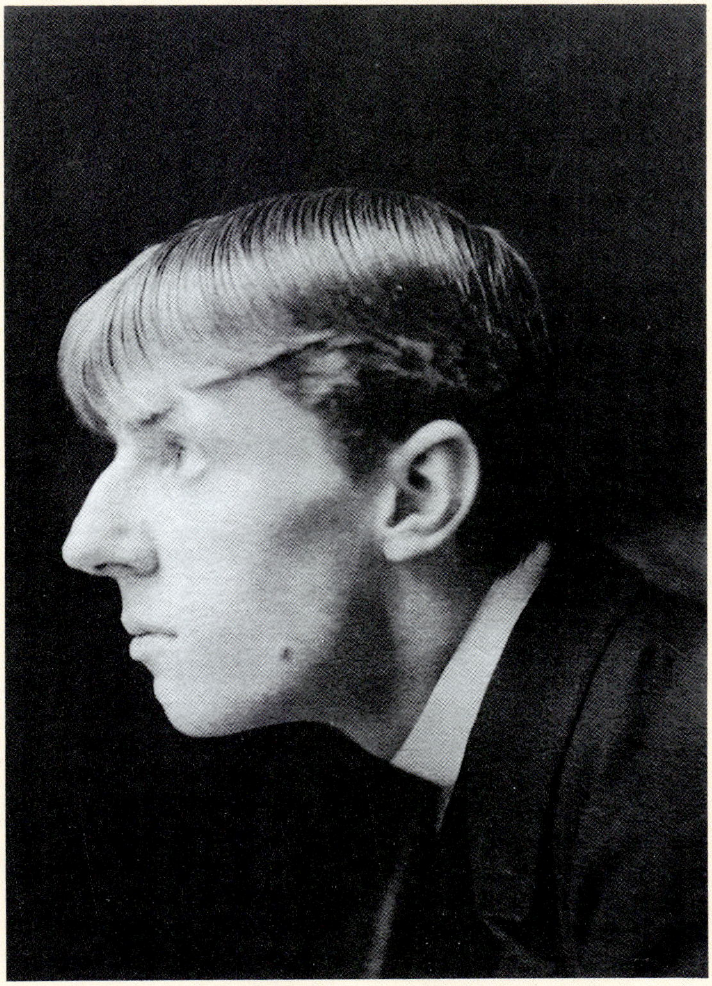

LEFT

A photograph of Beardsley taken in 1895 by Frederick Evans who also owned a bookshop in Cheapside in the City of London. Beardsley was a regular customer and the two became friends. It was Evans who introduced Beardsley to the publisher John Dent who was looking for an artist to illustrate the medieval English version of *Le Morte d'Arthur*. This was Beardsley's first significant commission.

sample drawing eventually became the frontispiece to the second volume.

It was an enormous commission. In late 1892 Beardsley wrote to his old headmaster at Brighton Grammar, describing the scope of the undertaking. 'There will be 20 full page drawings . . . about 100 small drawings in the text, nearly 350 initial letters and the cover design. The drawings I have already done have met with the greatest approval from all who have seen them.'

GROTESQUERIE

In the same letter he also describes a further commission from Dent which was to run concurrently with his work on *Le Morte d'Arthur*. This was for a series of 60 small drawings, or vignettes, to illustrate three volumes of *Bon-Mots*, collections of sayings by noted wits and bon viveurs, including the poet Richard Sheridan and the humorist Sydney Smith. Beardsley described

RIGHT
Beardsley's sense of the grotesque – an artistic convention which deliberately plays upon forms which are exaggeratedly bizarre and ugly – can be traced back to early Italian Renaissance painters such as Carlo Crivelli.

RIGHT
One of the calligraphic fantasies in a grotesque vein Beardsley created to illustrate the Bon-Mots of poet Richard Sheridan and humorist Sydney Smith. This is the first appearance of the strange foetus-like creature which was to figure in many of Beardsley's later works.

these drawings as '. . . tiny little things, some not more than an inch high, and the pen strokes to be counted on the fingers'.

Most are calligraphic fantasies in a grotesque vein, to which Beardsley's fine line style of drawings was particularly well suited. The use of the grotesque, which deliberately plays upon forms which are exaggerated bizarre and ugly, is an accepted artistic convention, and an important element in much of Beardsley's work. It tends to express a particularly disillusioned view of life, and this underpinned Beardsley's occasionally morbid philosophical outlook. In one famous remark he declared that: 'I have one thing – the grotesque. If I am not grotesque, then I am nothing.'

In one drawing from the *Bon-Mots* of Smith and Sheridan, a strange, foetus-like creature, which was to feature in many of his later works, appears for the first time. Other *Bon-Mots* drawings show the influences of his trip to Paris – the poster-like composition of the French lithographer Jules Cheret, and the recurring image of the human eye as a spider, first used by the Symbolist painter Odilon Redon.

The complete set of *Bon-Mots* vignettes took Beardsley a mere 10 days to complete, an indication of the feverish pace at which he was inclined to work. He was paid £15 for the *Bon-Mots*, and eventually received £250 for the *Le Morte d'Arthur* illustrations. These commissions finally enabled Beardsley to forsake the daily drudgery of the insurance office, and towards the end of 1882 he wrote: 'I left the fire office about two months ago, to the greatest satisfaction of said office and myself. If there ever was a case of the square boy in the round hole, it was mine.'

OPPOSITE RIGHT *The Achieving of the Sangreal* from *Le Morte d'Arthur*. This was a sample illustration which Beardsley prepared for John Dent in order to secure the commission. The drawing uses a conventional line and wash technique as opposed to the flat black and white tones of Beardsley's later illustrations. The abundance of detail was also to be drastically pared down.

RIGHT AND BELOW Two more thumbnail vignettes from the *Bon-Mots* series.

THE *MORTE d'ARTHUR* ILLUSTRATIONS

For the next year or so Beardsley was preoccupied with producing illustrations for *Le Morte d'Arthur*. The book itself was published in 12 parts between June 1893 and November 1894, in an ordinary edition of 1,500 copies at 2s 6d each, and a special edition on Dutch handmade paper of 300 copies at 6s 6d each. When the issue was complete, the purchaser could return the parts to the publisher for a casebinding, also designed by Beardsley. The ordinary edition was bound into two volumes, the handmade paper edition into three. The cover for the casebinding of *Le Morte d'Arthur* is one of Beardsley's greatest single works. The design is truly extraordinary, in its balance of elegantly controlled composition, and the lush effect of the huge, fleshy *fleurs du mal* with their scythe-like leaves, writhing in serpentine curves across the surface of the cover.

This expressive power was also translated to the illustrations. To begin with, Beardsley depended heavily on his assimilation of existing motifs and mannerisms, especially those of Burne-Jones, Walter Crane and William Morris. He gradually developed his pure black and white illustrative style, however, giving it a rich, medieval flavour that was both decorative and expressive.

If a page from *Le Morte d'Arthur* is compared with an illustration from one of William Morris's Kelmscott books which Beardsley was supposed to be imitating, the distance he had travelled from the restrained and careful medievalism of Morris is clear. The tranquil and delicate foliage of Morris's borders is replaced by twisting briar twigs and powerful organic plant forms, pulsating with life. Moreover, the figures of Burne-Jones, no more than decorative cyphers, have been deposed by a group of sinister female fauns, endowed with alternatively evil and ecstatic expressions, climbing in and out of the threatening foliage.

A mutual friend of Beardsley and Morris, the designer Aymer Valance, made the mistake of showing William Morris a printed proof of one of Beardsley's drawings for *Le Morte d'Arthur*, in an attempt to interest the great man in this rising new talent. Perhaps not surprisingly, Morris took an intense dislike to Beardsley's

HOW SIR TRISTRAM
DRANK OF THE
LOVE DRINK

work, largely on account of his use of mechanical reproduction methods, and remarked, somewhat caustically, that 'a man ought to do his own work'. He was also irritated, and quite possibly disturbed, by the imitation and transmogrification of the Kelmscott style. Beardsley's modernist approach had brought about a startling change and corruption of Morris's ideal, medieval dream world – a world which, in Beardsley's hands, had emphatically lost its innocence.

LEFT
How Sir Tristram drank of the Love Drink – one of the most brilliantly evocative illustrations from the *Le Morte d'Arthur* series. The starting point is the emotional climax of the story when Sir Tristram drinks a potion prepared by Isoud which he believes to be poison but is in fact a love potion. The weaving together of love and death into a single dramatic theme is one of the most powerful devices in romantic art, and one which held a particular fascination for Beardsley.

Beardsley reported Morris's reaction in a letter: 'William Morris has sworn a terrible oath against me for daring to bring out a book in this manner,' adding significantly, and not without a hint of youthful brashness, that 'the truth is that, while his work is a mere imitation of the old stuff, mine is fresh and original.'

The complete set of drawings for *Le Morte d'Arthur* provide a fascinating insight into the maturing of Beardsley's powers of design and draughtsmanship, which achieved a new measure of sophistication as the series progressed. One of the earliest illustrations, *How King Arthur saw the Questing Beast*, is also one of the most elaborate, executed in Beardsley's 'hair line' manner, a technique originally used for his simple drawing, *The Achieving of the Sangreal*. However, this elaborate style was later superseded by the use of pure black and white masses, which proved better suited to the lineblock reproduction process.

In *How King Arthur saw the Questing Beast* there is a profusion of detail decorating every part of the landscape, and each element is overlaid with calligraphic flourishes. The beast itself is a pseudo-Japanese dragon, its overlapping discs representing scales, and apparently derived from the scale-like decoration used by Whistler in the Peacock Room. The lines defining King Arthur's garments imitate the gouging of the needle on copperplate in a 15th century engraving. The precise castle in the background reveals how Beardsley was still entranced by the legend he was illustrating.

This drawing also marks the first appearance of Beardsley's new signature in the bottom right-hand corner – a device consisting of three vertical lines and three arrows or heart-shaped forms. It is obviously inspired by Whistler's stylized butterfly signature, and the intention of both designs was to avoid written words interfering with the pictorial purity of the overall composition.

Many of the early illustrations for *Le Morte d'Arthur* reveal the influence of Walter Crane, but it was not long before Beardsley abandoned such archaisms. In one of the smaller designs for a chapter heading, his true instincts begin to manifest themselves. In this illustration, used repeatedly throughout the series, a winged heraldic beast surmounts the recumbent body of a fallen angel,

OPPOSITE RIGHT
How La Belle Isoud nursed Sir Tristram. This depicts an early encounter between Tristram and Isoud, in which Beardsley evokes Isoud's dawning passion as she tends to the wounded knight. The theme of passion held in check is echoed by the formal structure of the composition which contrasts with the flame-like border designed to express the powerful natural forces gathering beneath the outwardly severe surface of the two lovers.

RIGHT
Chapter heading from *Le Morte d'Arthur.* The composition is reminiscent of a Japanese print, and the design is strikingly Art Nouveau.

who supports his head with his hands, wearing a flippant expression of resigned worry. It is hard to imagine any artist but Beardsley deliberately giving such an expression to an angel.

The influence of Burne-Jones can also be discerned in the early drawings. In *Merlin and Nimue*, for example, the figure of Merlin seems to have been based on Beardsley's remembrance of the pilgrim in the picture *Love leading the Pilgrim* by Burne-Jones, although the form of Merlin still owes a debt to the style of early woodcuts. Other elements in the composition display a Burne-Jones iconographical history, but are rendered more broadly and boldly. The honeysuckle border has as much rigidity Beardsley was able to reconcile with his essentially serpentine instincts.

In the late summer of 1893, Beardsley eventually discovered his métier, with the execution of two highly impressive full page drawings illustrating the legend of Sir Tristram and La Beale Isoud. This portion of *Le Morte d'Arthur* occupies barely a third of the first volume, but Beardsley devoted five full page drawings to it, out of a total of 12 in that volume. This is almost certainly because he was already fascinated by the story, which had been elaborated into a more romanticized form by Wagner in his opera, *Tristan und Isolde* (first performed 1865).

HOW LA BEALE
ISOVD NVRSED
SIR TRISTRAM

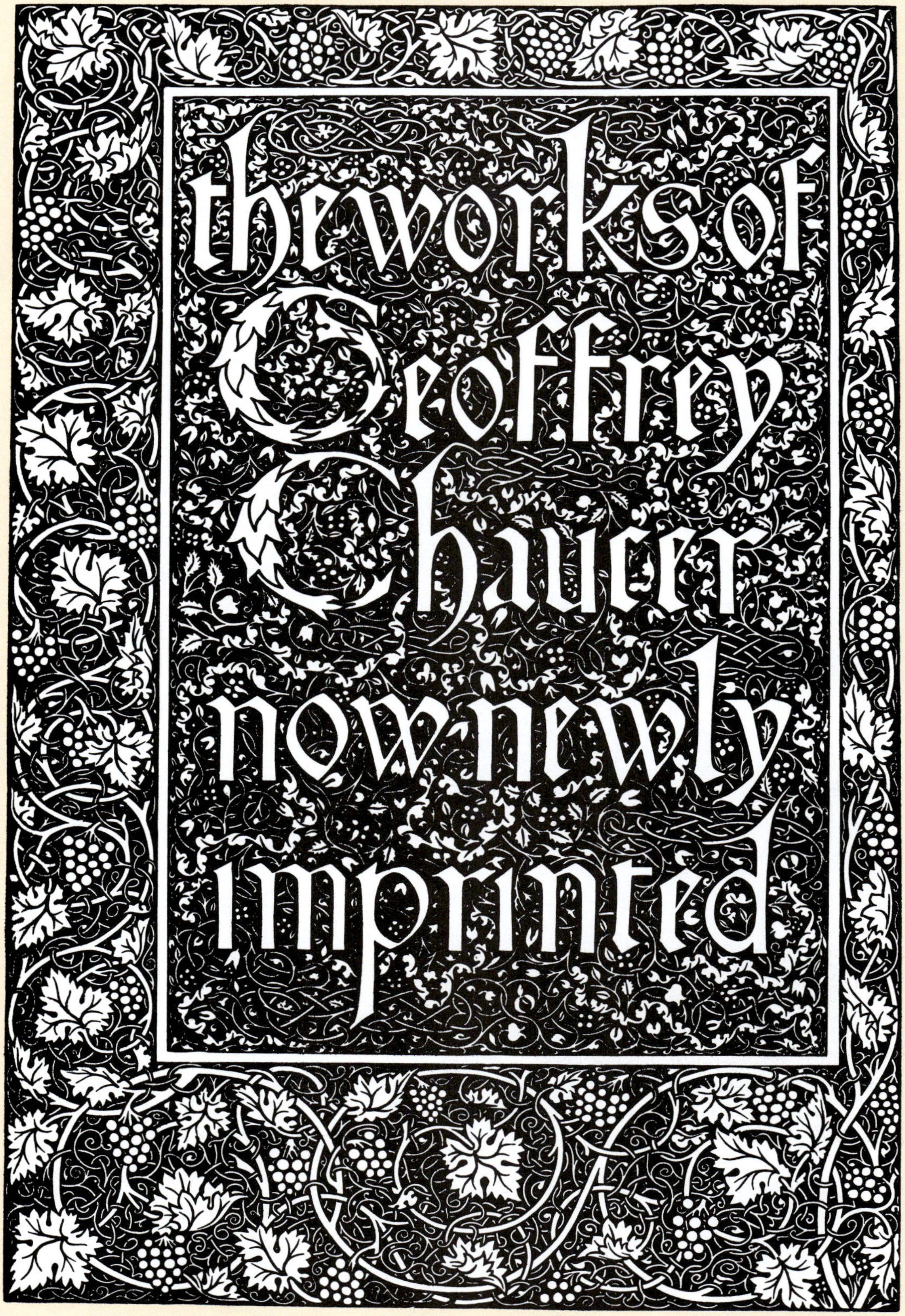
the works of
Geoffrey
Chaucer
now newly
imprinted

OPPOSITE LEFT

A page from the Kelmscott Chaucer designed by William Morris. Beardsley used Morris's richly decorative medieval illustrative style as a starting point for *Le Morte d'Arthur*, but infused his drawings with a potent, sinister quality which, not surprisingly, outraged Morris.

LEFT

How King Arthur Saw the Questing Beast. An illustration for *Le Morte* in Beardsley's original highly wrought linear style. This later gave way to simplified black and white areas of tone which were suited to the technical demands of the line block reproduction process.

MERLIN AND
NIMVE

OPPOSITE LEFT
Merlin and Ninwe, a full page illustration from *Le Morte d'Arthur*. The sinuous curving foliage of the border is one of the earliest examples of Art Nouveau design.

LEFT
Design for a chapter heading in *Le Morte d'Arthur*. This is one of the last drawings in the series and shows that Beardsley had finally become disenchanted with the commission to the extent that he abandons any attempt to clothe the figure in medieval fashion. The sheer volume of the workload eventually took its toll.

In the drawing *How La Beale Isoud Nursed Sir Tristram*, Beardsley brilliantly evokes Isoud's dawning passion, as she tends to the wounded knight. Equally impressive is the way in which the theme of passion held in check is echoed by the formal structure of the composition. The two figures, rendered with extreme economy, are firmly contained within a grid of lines, typical of certain types of Japanese prints. By contrast, Beardsley unleashes a continuous growth of flame-like tree forms in the border, clearly designed to express the powerful natural forces gathering beneath the apparently calm surface of the two lovers.

In the other key drawing, Beardsley takes as his starting point the emotional climax of the story, when Sir Tristram drinks a potion prepared by Isoud which he believes to be poison, but which is in fact a love potion substituted by one of Isoud's servants. Beardsley captures perfectly Isoud's expression of bitter triumph as she watches Tristram prepare to drink, and the strong perspective of the floorboards gives dramatic support to the tension of this scene of idealized love. The weaving together of love and death into a single theme is one of the most powerful devices in romantic art, and one which held a particular fascination for Beardsley.

ABOVE AND ABOVE RIGHT
Heavy woodcut black line and fine Art Nouveau curves of chapter heading illustrations for *Le Morte D'Arthur*.

OPPOSITE RIGHT
The final full page illustration for *Le Morte d'Arthur* depicting Queen Guinever's retreat into a monastery. The black mass of her cloak creates a distinctly sinister atmosphere.

However, the sheer volume of the *Morte d'Arthur* commission eventually began to take its toll. Towards the end of the series Beardsley was becoming bored and tired of his work, and the resulting designs show a marked tendency towards bold simplification, with the clothes of some of his figures showing characteristics of the late 19th century instead of the Middle Ages. One notable exception to this creeping artistic *ennui* is the final full page illustration, which depicts Queen Guinever's retreat into a monastery. Beardsley stresses Guinever's character as an adultress and femme fatale, giving her the features of a pretty, sensual young woman, but he adds a sinister touch in the raven's beak silhoutte of the cowl of her nun's habit. This drawing provides an enigmatic clue to Beardsley's evolving powers of design, and represents probably the best early example of the mysterious massed black shapes that were to become a feature of his mature style.

WORK FOR THE ART MAGAZINES AND SALOMÉ: 'THAT INVISIBLE DANCE'

Towards the end of 1892, another great opportunity presented itself to Beardsley. He was introduced to Lewis Hind, who at that

OPPOSITE LEFT
The Peacock Skirt, an early illustration for Oscar Wilde's play *Salomé*. The fragmented peacock tail design was based on Whistler's decorated screens in *The Peacock Room*.

LEFT
The Man in the Moon from *Salomé*. This has always been considered one of the most perfect of all Beardsley's works, an impressive example of his ability to create powerful expressive effects with extreme economy and purity of line. The face of the moon is a caricature of Oscar Wilde, the play's author.

time was the sub-editor of *The Art Journal*, but who was planning to launch his own art magazine, *The Studio*. He was looking for something exceptional for the first issue, and in Beardsley's work he found it. Hind commissioned the distinguished critic, etcher and biographer of Whistler, Joseph Pennell, to write an appraisal of Beardsley's work, and commissioned Beardsley himself to design the cover of the new magazine.

The first issue of *The Studio* duly appeared in April 1893. It contained Pennell's article, *Aubrey Beardsley – A New Illustrator* together with eight examples of his work, including *Madame Cigale*, *Les Revenants de Musique* and two pages from *Le Morte d'Arthur*, which formed a complete conspectus of Beardsley's output to date. Pennell's article proved to be as perceptive as his

OPPOSITE RIGHT
The Stomach Dance from *Salomé*. Beardsley conceives of Salomé as an exotic, oriental belly dancer, with the seven veils billowing out from between her thighs. The flame-haired musician is another example of grotesque creatures.

RIGHT
The Dancer's Reward. This illustrates one of the climactic moments in the play when Salomé is presented with the head of John the Baptist.

choice of drawings, describing Beardsley as '. . . an artist whose work is quite remarkable in its execution as it is in its invention, a very rare combination.'

He was also aware of Beardsley's ability to create an original style from a synthesis of many traditional elements: '. . . it is quite impossible to say what his style may be . . . he has not been carried back into the 15th century, or succumbed to the limits of Japan; he has recognised that he is living in the last decade of the 19th century.'

The appearance of *The Studio* further stimulated the public interest in Beardsley that had been steadily growing since his meeting with Dent in 1892. Beardsley was well aware of the excitement he was generating, as an extract from a letter written in February 1893 shows: 'Behold me, then, the coming man, the rage of artistic London, the admired of all schools, the besought of publishers, the subject of articles . . . I have fortune at my feet . . . and I have really more work on my hands than I can possibly get through and have to refuse all sorts of nice things.'

One thing Beardsley certainly did not refuse was his next major commission from the publisher John Lane at The Bodley Head publishers to illustrate Oscar Wilde's play *Salomé*. This arose directly out of the publication in *The Studio* of a drawing entitled *J'ai Baisé ta Bouche, Iokanaan* which was, fact, an illustration to

OPPOSITE LEFT
The Eyes of Herod, a full page illustration from *Salomé*. Beardsley expresses King Herod's fatal lust through a multitude of phallic symbols – candles, peacocks' heads, trees. The overall composition is of great decorative splendour yet charged with a lascivious intensity.

LEFT
Tailpiece from *Salomé*.

Salomé done quite spontaneously by Beardsley after reading the play. Wilde had written *Salomé* in French, and it was published simultaneously in Paris and London on February 22, 1893. Some time in March Wilde sent a copy of this first edition to Beardsley with the following dedication – 'March 1893. For Aubrey: for the only artist who, beside myself, knows what the dance of the seven veils is, and can see that invisible dance. Oscar.'

This inscription clearly suggests that Wilde sensed a strong affinity between Beardsley's work and his own play, and his instincts proved to be correct. Beardsley eagerly devoured *Salomé*, and responded by crystallizing its central image, the climactic moment when a triumphant Salomé embraces the severed head of John the Baptist. This was the drawing which was originally published in the first issue of *The Studio*, and was subsequently reworked to form part of a group of illustrations which collectively constitute Beardsley's greatest achievement, in terms of expressive quality, inventiveness and stylistic originality.

The *Salomé* drawings, executed between May and November of 1893, were the last of Beardsley's early works. They were novel at the time, and still retain the power to amaze, largely because the compositions are unique as abstract patterns and because the sense of drama conveyed by the designs is so intense. The use of flat planes of pure black and white, linked by lines which vary in strength, suggests something of the frozen, transfixed quality characteristic of a bas-relief. It is not surprising to learn that during this time Beardsley's art was enhanced and influenced by his study of the paintings on 5th-century Grecian vases, found at the British Museum in London.

The relationship between Wilde and Beardsley was a curious one, and the subject of much speculation. Most commentators agree that having received the commission for *Salomé*, Beardsley's initial enthusiasm for Wilde gradually cooled. Although they had many artistic and intellectual interests in common, it was quite possible that Wilde, then at the arrogant height of his powers, patronized Beardsley, implying that he was rising to fame as a mere satellite of Wilde's poetic genius. Beardsley, whose favourite authors were Ben Johnson and Racine, and who had a highly developed sense of what constituted good literature, must have recognized the deficiencies of *Salomé* and realized that it would be remembered only as a pretext for his illustrations.

But whatever Beardsley may have felt about the literary merits of *Salomé*, he accepted it as a source of inspiration, and it proved the ideal pretext for exploiting his sense of evil. In the drawing entitled *Enter Herodias*, a showman whose face is a mischievous caricature of Oscar Wilde, introduces Herodias, the mother of Salomé. She is portrayed as the epitome of an evil matriarch, rising above her two degenerate companions with authentic satanic majesty. The strange dwarfish attendant who holds back Herodias's cloak is the same foetus-like creature which appeared in earlier illustrations to the series of *Bon-Mots*.

During this period of the *Salomé* drawings, Beardsley was at his most provocative, introducing overt erotic elements into his work which he knew would shock. This caused considerable trouble with the publisher, John Lane, who insisted on censoring several of the original illustrations. In the case of *Enter Herodias*, Lane objected to the nudity of the slave boy, and Beardsley was obliged to erase the offending parts from the original drawing, and replace them with a slightly flippant fig leaf.

One of the most bitter controversies erupted over Beardsley's initial attempt at illustrating *The Toilet of Salomé*. Lane objected strenuously to the depiction of a youth on a Moorish stool, clearly indulging in auto-eroticism as he gazes at a naked boy with a coffee tray. Also scattered around Salomé's dressing table were several 'bibles' of the Decadent movement – Baudelaire's *Les Fleurs du Mal*, and Zola's Realist novel *La Terre*, which was con-

RIGHT

Enter Herodias. At this period in the *Salomé* series, Beardsley was at his most provocative, peppering his drawings with overtly erotic references. The page boy in this scene was originally depicted nude, until a publisher's objection forced Beardsley to insert a jokey fig leaf. The drawing portrays the entrance of Herodias, Salomé's mother, and Beardsley has created an unforgettable image of this evil matriarch. The master of ceremonies is yet another caricature of Oscar Wilde.

SALO

sidered pornographic in England and had been the subject of a prosecution in 1888.

Unperturbed, Beardsley went on to make a second version of *The Toilet*, which is undoubtedly a more purely beautiful drawing than the original, and features a new hard-edged abstraction in the frail, densely black furniture, and the linear evocation of essential details. The two versions of *The Toilet of Salomé* ostensibly illustrate the scene in the play where Salomé is prepared for her dance in front of King Herod, indicated by the stage direction: 'Slaves bring perfume and the seven veils, and take the sandals off Salomé.'

LEFT
The Toilet of Salomé. One of the most famous drawings in the series depicts the scene when Salomé is prepared for the dance by her slaves. This is the second version – the original was considered too offensive by the publisher.

Beardsley uses this as an excuse to elaborate entirely personal fantasies on a theme which constantly fascinated him – a woman seen in the intimacies of her personal toilet.

For the dance itself, Beardsley depicts Salomé as an oriental belly dancer, with some of the seven veils apparently floating out from between her thighs. Salomé is accompanied in her dance by a grotesque, flame-haired musician, who clearly shows the effect of her erotic dancing in another provocative tableau.

The most climactic moments occur towards the end of the play, where Salomé first receives the head of John the Baptist, and then holds it up and embraces it. For these scenes Beardsley produced two stunning compositions. In *The Dancer's Reward*, he takes his cue from Wilde's stage direction: 'A huge black arm, the arm of the Executioner comes forth from the cistern bearing on a silver shield the head of John. Salomé seizes it.'

Beardsley brilliantly depicts Salomé's expression of savage incredulity at the fulfilment of her impossible desire, and she even touches the blood with her fingertips, as if to make sure she is not dreaming. In *The Climax*, Salomé seizes the head of John and harangues it in a long, passionate and tragic speech. Much of the power of this scene and its great appeal for Beardsley comes from the explicit emergence of the great romantic theme of intermingled love and death, also explored in *Le Morte d'Arthur*.

Wilde then carries the play through to its logical conclusion. Salomé reiterates the words that Beardsley inscribed in their original French on the first version of this drawing – 'I have kissed thy mouth, Jokanaan' – and King Herod, disgusted, gives orders to kill her. The stage direction which follows reads: 'The soldiers rush forward and crush beneath their shields. Salomé, daughter of Herodias, princess of Judea. Curtain.'

CHAPTER THREE

WORKS FOR THE JOURNALS THE YELLOW BOOK & THE SAVOY

FOLLOWING the completion of *Salomé*, Beardsley turned away from the fantastical Biblical world of Oscar Wilde and the remote medievalism of *Le Morte d'Arthur*, both of which had exercised such a powerful imaginative sway on him, and returned to the development of his own vision of life, art and literature. The next distinct phase of his brief, dazzling career began with the work he completed for *The Yellow Book*; described by Beardsley as 'a new literary and artistic quarterly', it was the brainchild of himself and his friend Henry Harland. Harland was an American writer who came to London in 1889, and quickly established a foothold in the avant garde artistic circle which revolved around his fellow American, the painter James McNeill Whistler.

'Our idea,' wrote Beardsley in January 1894, 'is that many brilliant story painters and picture writers cannot get their best stuff accepted in the conventional magazines, either because they are not topical or perhaps a little too risqué.'

Beardsley and Whistler took their idea to John Lane, who had published *Salomé*. He was suitably impressed with their proposal and agreed to act as publisher. Henry Harland was appointed literary editor and Beardsley art editor. The first issue was planned to appear on April 15, 1894.

'REPULSIVENESS AND INSOLENCE'

The boom years of 1893 to 1894 produced many periodicals, most of which disappeared within a few months, but *The Yellow Book* was to be different – a properly bound quarterly, with flaunting yellow covers, the colour of ordinary French novels, which at the time were simply bound in yellow paper. More importantly, it intended to challenge the current vested interests in art and literature, and there is no doubt that Beardsley, and to a lesser extent, Harland, wanted *The Yellow Book* to be, in Beardsley's words 'a little risqué'.

The fact is, however, that the majority of the contributors were

RIGHT

The arrival of *The Yellow Book* magazine signalled a new phase in Beardsley's artistic development, essentially a more direct commentary on contemporary life, but always seen in terms of Beardsley's own particular vision. The girl depicted in the cover design for the first issue is a creature of the night, an habitué of the opera, cafés, bars and theatre. The disappearing pierrot in the background is thought to be a caricature of Elkin Matthews, co-publisher of *The Yellow Book*, who disapproved of both its style and content.

THE YELLOW BOOK
AN ILLVSTRATED QVARTERLY.
BOOKS
PRICE
FIVE SHILLINGS
ELKIN MATHEWS
AND JOHN LANE.
THE BODLEY HEAD
VIGO ST. LONDON.
APRIL 15th
MDCCCXCIV.

The Yellow Book
An Illustrated Quarterly
Volume II July 1894
London: Elkin Mathews & John Lane
Boston: Copeland & Day
Price
5/-
Net

LEFT
Beardsley's designs for *The Yellow Book* covers introduced a new illustrative style which featured heavy black masses. The woman has a characteristic air of sensual depravity.

LEFT
The new boldness of Beardsley's illustrative style was particularly effective when combined with the garish yellow paper of the *Yellow Book* covers.

eminently respectable. The first two items in Volume I, after Beardsley's cover and title page, were a drawing by the President of The Royal Academy, Lord Leighton, and a short story by the American novelist Henry James. It was almost solely Beardsley's contributions which gave *The Yellow Book* its character and so-called 'decadent' reputation, which precipitated the outraged reaction of the press. *The Times* referred to the 'repulsiveness and insolence' of the cover, and went on to describe the publication as 'a combination of English rowdyism and French lubricity'. It was two of the illustrations in the first issue – *Mrs Patrick Campbell* and *L'Éducation Sentimentale* – which galvanized *The Westminster Gazette* into making its now famous remark: 'We do not know that anything would meet the case except a short Act of Parliament to make this kind of thing illegal'.

It is hard to understand why Beardsley's accomplished and apparently restrained caricature of the actress Mrs Patrick Campbell was found so offensive. It seems to have been partly due to

RIGHT
The Fat Women. Classically ordered in composition in spite of its small scale, this is one of Beardsley's greatest drawings. It shows a woman sitting at a café table, almost certainly The Café Royal in London, a favourite haunt of artists and writers. She is a marvellous example of the 'demi-mondaines' who populated Beardsley's art at this time

the sheer economy of the drawing style, which gave the figure an extremely ephemeral appearance. The shock caused by the illustration inspired by Gustave Flaubert's novel, *L'Éducation Sentimentale*, is much more understandable. In this case, the theme is evidently the corruption of youth by experience, although a close inspection of the young girl suggests that she is already far from innocent.

Despite the storm of moral outrage caused by its publication, there is no doubt that the first four issues of *The Yellow Book* were a phenomenal success. It was widely advertised and rapidly bought, attracting praise and vilification in equally ferocious measure. Several editions were published, an unusual occurrence in periodical literature at the time. In each issue Beardsley managed to produce some startling, mordant, bitter or freshly beautiful design.

The covers alone were enough to arrest the man in the street, as indeed they were meant to do, with their thick, black, sensuous lines on bright yellow, the colour that had become the hallmark

LEFT
This naturalistic study of a group of waiters at The Café Royal shows that Beardsley could observe and record real human beings if he wanted to. The juxtaposition of white and black masses is a remarkable piece of design.

of the daring French novel. The choice of imagery was also highly suggestive. On the cover of Volume I, a dark mephistophelian man strikes a sinister note behind the robust figure of a masked woman, and on the second issue, published in July 1894, Beardsley presents the stylized profile of a young woman, whose thick lips and abundant hair suggest erotic emancipation typical of the anti-genteel style of late Victorian women.

This type of figure also features in a design for the front cover of a prospectus for *The Yellow Book* which was widely circulated prior to the launch. The girl in this drawing is a modern version of the depraved, sensual women from history and myth that Beardsley had depicted in the past. An actress, singer, dancer, courtesan or woman of the night, her domain is the theatre, opera, cafés and bars of London's West End. The comic and slightly crusty-looking Pierrot bookseller is said to be a caricature of John Lane's partner, Elkin Matthews, who, compared to Lane, was somewhat prudish and viewed the entire Yellow Book publishing enterprise with undisguised apprehension and disapproval.

RIGHT
Beardsley's predilection for 'fantastic conceptions' remained undiminished, as this illustration for the *Comedy Ballet of the Marionettes* clearly shows. The heroine is being simultaneously courted by her cuckolded husband, and a stylishly attired lesbian.

RIGHT
The black masses of the dwarf's turban and the lesbian's dress contrast with the linear purity of this illustration, the second in the series for *The Comedy Ballet of the Marionettes.*

Throughout his Yellow Book period, Beardsley's work can be seen as having some parallel with that of Henri de Toulouse-Lautrec's scenes of the Parisian 'demi-monde'. Beardsley's drawings are characterized by a mood of involvement in the life of the late 19th century, in contrast to his previous stylistic forays into the realms of medievalism and mythology.

As always, however, this world is seen in terms of Beardsley's own particular artistic and personal obsessions, and his predilection for 'fantastic conceptions' remained undiminished. A sequence of drawings made for the second volume of *The Yellow Book*, entitled *The Comedy Ballet of The Marionettes*, are populated by a grotesque mixture of dwarfs, lesbians and cuckolded husbands all converging on a ravishing heroine in 18th-century dress. But Beardsley could observe real human beings when he wanted to – the same volume contains *Les Garcons du Café*

REJANE

Royal, based on actual experience. The contrasting physical types of the waiters is highly convincing, and the movement of the black masses of their jackets interrupted by the white of the plates and napkins is a remarkable piece of design.

The third volume of *The Yellow Book* was published in October 1894, by which time Elkin Matthews's reservations had got the better of him, and he had parted company with John Lane. Beardsley, however, continued to chronicle the excitements of London life with happy defiance. Volume 3 contains one of his most evocative illustrations, *The Wagnerites,* which also demonstrates a newly-evolved drawing style. In a reversal of his previous practice, he conjures up form with small areas of white set in great masses of black. These white areas were obtained simply by leaving the paper devoid of ink, a technique which required immense skill on the part of the artist. In the case of *The Wagnerites*, however, Beardsley was obliged to resort to some retouching with Chinese white.

LEFT
Madame Rejane, the French actress, appeared in London in 1894. Beardsley developed a fervent admiration for her and depicted her in a number of media. This is one of Beardsley's most exquisite works, and shows how little after all, his work was dependent on diabolism.

The drawing itself depicts a bizarre audience, composed entirely of depraved and ugly-looking women, surrounding a single insignificant man. It seems more than likely that Beardsley was satirizing those wealthy and worldly opera goers for whom the opera is simply another part of the fashionable social round. Beardsley himself was a cultivated opera buff, and his deliberate signposting of *Tristan und Isolde*, Wagner's homage to the idyll of romantic love, is intended to form a poignant contrast with the grossness of the audience.

This satirizing of high society is also apparent in *Lady Gold's Escort*, which depicts a fragile but undoubtedly well-heeled woman surrounded by a leering scrum of men in various stages of depravity, with billowing white shirts, top hats and baggy trousers. The drawing technique is the same used in *The Wagnerites*, with black masses predominating. The original stimulus to this phase of Beardsley's development was probably his appreciation of the poetic qualities of Whistler's *Nocturnes*, only in Beardsley's hands the pitch-black darkness became genuinely sinister, even when portraying a relatively innocuous subject, such as a woman at her dressing table in *La Dame aux Camelias*. Here a solid black mass envelops the lower half of the room, and seems about to consume the female figure.

The third volume of *The Yellow Book* also included a memorable self-portrait of Beardsley, in which he visualizes himself in a huge turbanned nightcap, lying alone in an ornate four poster bed. The drawing is inscribed with the words '*Par les dieux jumeaux, tous les monstres ne sont pas en Afrique*'.

LEFT

This illustration entitled *The Mysterious Rose Garden* appears at first glance to be an impious parody of the Annunciation, but Beardsley reworks a traditional image to give it fresh impetus.

RIGHT

La Dame aux Camelias shows a woman at her dressing table, a favourite Beardsley theme.

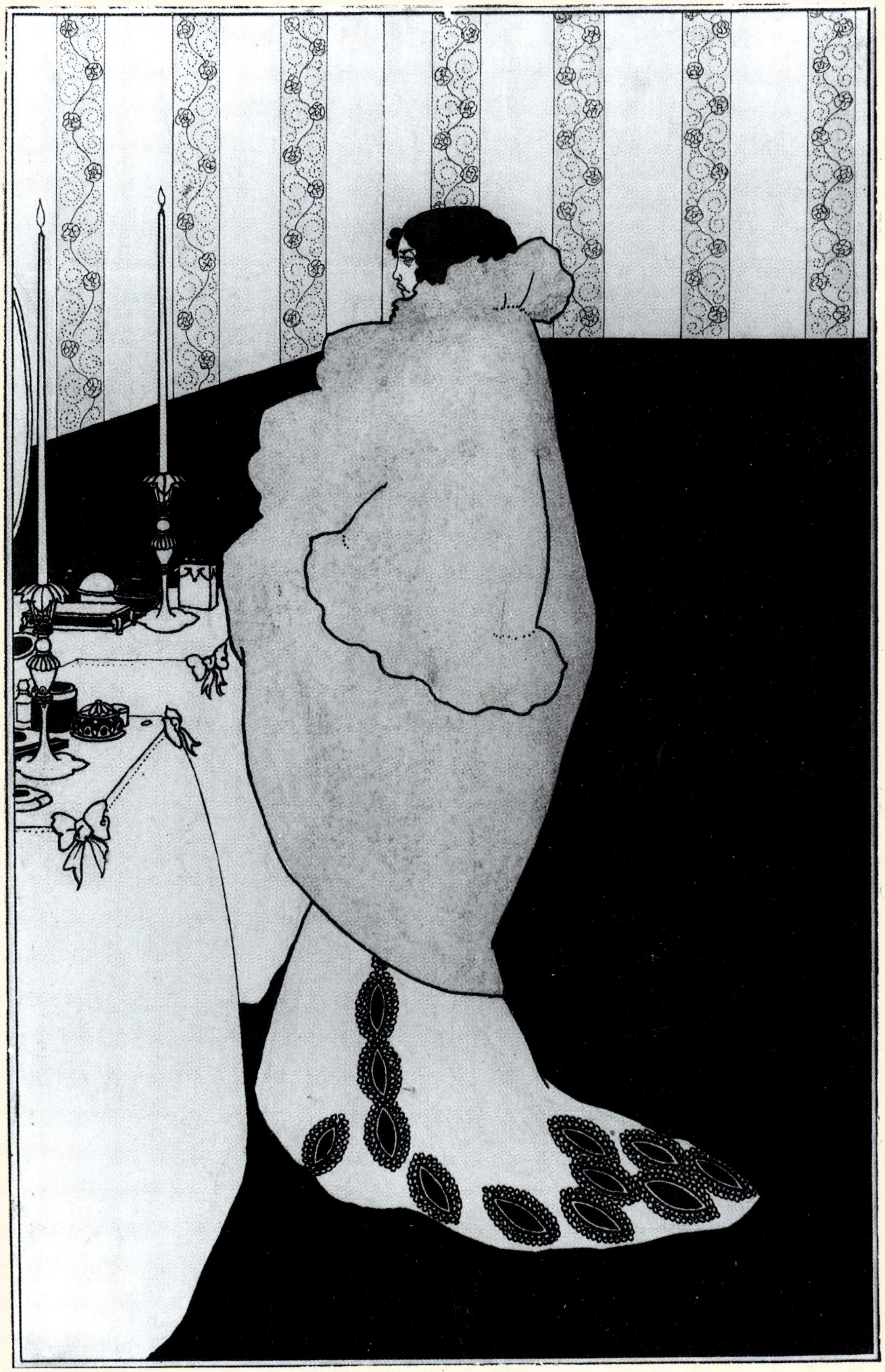

This designation of himself by implication as some kind of monster was a rationalization of his early feelings at school, and later on in life, that he was markedly different from those around him, and therefore somehow grotesque. By this time, however, he had learned to take a gleeful pride in the difference, as this drawing wittily shows.

The fourth volume of *The Yellow Book* appeared in January 1895. It included an illustration entitled *The Mysterious Rose Garden*, which at first glance appears to be an impious parody of the Annunciation – Beardsley himself referred to it as the first in a series of illustrations to the Bible. But to see it merely as a parody or burlesque is too simplistic – here Beardsley reworks an important and powerful traditional image, and gives it fresh significance. The flat, virginal body of the young girl is contrasted with the flame-fretted robe of the hermaphrodite messenger; the black lantern, which in some mysterious way gives an impression of light, is a strangely evil shape, promising to illuminate the darkest experiences.

As art editor of this by now publically notorious, but commercially successful publication, Beardsley's financial situation had improved to the extent that he and his sister Mabel could afford to buy a house at 114 Cambridge Street, Pimlico. The interior was striking – 'The walls of his room were distempered a violent orange, the doors and skirtings were painted black,' according to a description by the artist William Rothenstein.

With the acquisition of the house, the Beardsleys began a phase of 'being sociable' in the Victorian sense, by hosting tea parties which attracted a crowd of young writers and artists of *The Yellow Book* circle, including Oscar Wilde – who never actually contributed to the periodical – and a number of his friends. This period, from early 1894 to early 1895 is widely regarded as the time when Beardsley stamped his presence on the epoch and epitomized the spirit of the times. It is this moment that his friend and writer Max Beerbohm had in mind when he coined the phrase *The Beardsley Period.*

'THERE MUST BE AN ABSOLUTE END'

It all came to an abrupt and messy end in April 1895 when Oscar Wilde was arrested on a criminal charge of committing indecent acts, an event which Wilde's friend and biographer Frank Harris later described as 'the signal for an orgy of Philistine rancour such as even London had never known before'.

On the morning following Wilde's arrest, *The National Observer* declared in a leading article that to '. . . the Decadents, of their

ABOVE
This design for the fifth volume of *The Yellow Book* was withdrawn from publication during the scandal caused by the trial of Oscar Wilde, which eventually led to Beardsley's dismissal as art editor of *The Yellow Book*. Things were never to be the same.

hideous conception of the meaning of art, there must be an absolute end'.

The Yellow Book was by then an established benchmark of Decadence, and when Wilde was reported to have taken with him to prison the book he was reading when arrested – a yellow paper-covered French novel – several newspapers seized the opportunity to concoct the headline: 'arrest of Oscar Wilde Yellow Book under his arm'.

Beardsley was doubly vulnerable to this ferocious outburst of well-orchestrated indignation, since he was the art editor of *The Yellow Book* as well as the notorious illustrator of Oscar Wilde's *Salomé*. At the time of Wilde's arrest John Lane, the publisher of

LEFT

Atalanta in Calydon, one of the illustrations in the prospectus to the fifth issue of *The Yellow Book*, which was circulated prior to the Wilde controversy.

BELOW

Don Juan, Sganarelle and the Beggar. An illustration for Molière's play Don Juan which was published in *The Savoy*, the magazine started to fill the gap left by the disappearance of *The Yellow Book*.

The Yellow Book, was in the United States, but he soon began to receive telegrams from a number of his more respectable authors demanding Beardsley's dismissal. Beardsley was not a particular friend of Wilde's, and there is no firm evidence to suggest that he was a homosexual; but he was certainly unpopular, and, as the poet W B Yeats wrote later in an appraisal of the episode, 'the time had to come to get rid of unpopular persons .

Eventually John Lane received a cable from the poet William Watson which stated bluntly – 'Withdraw all Beardsley's designs or I withdraw all my books'. Lane became alarmed and sent instructions to his London office that all of Beardsley's work was to be removed from the fifth volume of *The Yellow Book*, then in preparation and about to go to press. This was duly done, and Beardsley was, in effect, dismissed from his post as art editor.

Lane's action later filled him with great remorse, and he came to regret deeply his hasty cowardice in bowing to public pressure. He kept all the irate telegrams from the Bodley Head authors, which are now displayed in the library at Princetown University, as a chastening monument to British hypocrisy.

As for *The Yellow Book* itself, it 'turned grey in a single night, though it lingered on, feeble and quite respectable for nine issues more', according to the writer E F Benson.

The last illustration by Beardsley to be published in *The Yellow Book* was a frontispiece to Juvenal's *Sixth Satire*. In this drawing, the profile of a grotesque old woman who could well have been one of *The Wagnerites*, is glimpsed as she is carried through the streets in an ornate sedan chair borne by two impassive monkey footmen. The buildings in the background bear little resemblance to ancient Rome, and instead echo the sweeping formality of Regency London and Brighton. Although this drawing was Beardsley's last published contribution to *The Yellow Book*, the prospectus for the fifth volume, which had been issued prior to the controversy, gives some indication of the proposed illustrations. These include a drawing of the mythological huntress *Atlanta in Calydon* and *A Chopin Nocturne*. The latter is wholly in sepia wash and line, and forms a companion to *Chopin Ballade 3*, an earlier drawing executed in a similar fashion with all the subtlety and economy of an early Japanese woodprint.

John Lane's telegram of dismissal arrived in April 1895. It not only caused Beardsley a great deal of mental and moral stress, but it also left him without any form of income. On April 20, Beardsley left the increasingly poisonous atmosphere of London and went to Paris, making a brief return visit a short time later with the aim of seeking advice from the writer and poet André

RIGHT
The Bathers pictured on the beach at Dieppe Beardsley succeeds in making the seaside look like a moonscape.

RIGHT
The Return of Tannhauser to the Venusberg. The drawing was intended to illustrate Beardsley's romantic novel, *The Story of Venus and Tannhauser* but it was never completed. The subject of Tannhauser's return, in pilgrim's clothes, to the realm of Venus fascinated Beardsley over the years and this particular design is one of his most moving.

Raffalovitch. Born in Paris in 1864 of wealthy Russian emigré parents, Raffalovitch had settled in London in 1882, and had become well known in literary circles through his propensity for lavish entertaining.

Although he had encountered Beardsley, the two men were not particularly great friends, so it must have been in some desperation that Beardsley turned to Raffalovitch for help. In the event he proved to be an unlikely saviour, for he undertook to provide the young artist with generous financial support, as well as instigating Beardsley's eventual conversion to the Catholic Church.

Raffalovitch was not Beardsley's only supporter in his last years, however. He had an unusual counterpart in the somewhat more pagan figure of Leonard Smithers, who was to succeed John Lane as Beardsley's publisher. Smithers was a remarkable man, a bibliophile solicitor from Yorkshire with no literary or artistic pretensions, who dealt in and published erotica together with avant garde literature. He was shrewd enough to perceive that money could be made out of high class pornography, and that Beardsley might prove a profitable investment. In accounts of Beardsley's life, Smithers has often been maligned, but he does deserve great credit for his support of Beardsley right up to the end, even when in severe financial difficulties himself.

THE SAVOY

Smithers's professional relationship with Beardsley began in the summer of 1895, following Beardsley's return from Paris in May. The English critic and poet Arthur Symons proposed that a new magazine should be started to take over the literary and artistic territory abandoned by *The Yellow Book* when it sacked Beardsley. Smithers was to be publisher, Symons the literary editor and Beardsley the art editor. The title, suggested by Beardsley, was to be *The Savoy*.

Smithers not only engaged Beardsley as art editor of the new publication, he also made an agreement to furnish Beardsley with a regular income of £25 per week, in return for his entire future output. This generous gesture restored some semblance of stability to Beardsley's chaotic existence, but his circumstances

and outlook had nonetheless been irrevocably changed by the consequences of the Wilde debacle. The London in which he had taken such delight and had reflected in his drawings would never be the same.

In July of 1895 Beardsley sold the black and orange house in Cambridge Street, and spent the summer flitting restlessly around Europe, visiting Dieppe, Cologne, Munich and Berlin. In October he returned to London, and settled in a suite of rented rooms which had once been used by Oscar Wilde. There he continued the work started in Dieppe on the first volume of *The Savoy*, which eventually appeared in January 1896.

RIGHT
Cover design for the first issue of *The Savoy* magazine, Beardsley's next publishing venture following the demise of *The Yellow Book*.

On the front cover of this first issue Beardsley added the small chubby figure of a *putto*, seemingly about to urinate on a copy of *The Yellow Book*. This detail was later excized for publication, but it clearly shows Beardsley's resentment at being abruptly ejected from the staff of the magazine eight months previously. The rest of the design is not particularly interesting, and it seems almost as if Beardsley had been temporarily deserted by the powers which had been his inspiration. In reality, this loss of intensity was partly due to Beardsley's rapidly deteriorating health and vision.

On the literary front, *The Savoy* was a general improvement on the standards set by *The Yellow Book*. Arthur Symons had a keener eye for quality than Henry Harland, and the literary section reflected his more astute judgement. In the literary milieu of *The Savoy*, Beardsley also became a writer, and several of his pieces were published, together with illustrations.

One of them, a poem called *The Ballad of a Barber*, was accompanied by one of Beardsley's most strikingly composed drawings which links up iconographically with the outline engravings of the Neo-classical artists of the Regency period. For all the richness of the background, the overall is suggestive not of a palace but a late Victorian suburban house. This makes the illustration all the more disturbing, because the barber's murderous act – he kills the little princess whose coiffure he has just finished – is thus rendered furtive and commonplace.

Beardsley's longest piece of prose writing is a so-called romantic novel entitled *Under the Hill*, a cleaner version of an extremely indecent original, *The Story of Venus and Tannhauser*, itself based on the German legend of Tannhauser. The first four chapters of *Under the Hill* were eventually published in volumes 1 and 2 of *The Savoy*.

Beardsley attached great importance to *Venus and Tannhauser* – the first reference to it occurs in a letter of 1894, and he was still working on it at the time of his death. It was clearly intended to be a

THE SAVOY
Nº 1.
JANUARY
1896
AUBREY BEARDSLEY. 1896.

major vehicle for the literary ambitions he never quite managed to relinquish. Although unfinished, it constitutes a minor masterpiece – a quintessentially 'Decadent' work which has ultimately assured Beardsley of the place in literary history he so coveted.

ROCOCO

LEFT
The Abbé, an illustration for Beardsley's rococo novel *Under the Hill*. This marks the start of a more decorative, linear illustrative style which was inspired by 18th century France.

Beardsley's designs for *The Savoy* – and his illustrations for *Under the Hill* in particular – mark a dramatic new development in his art. This was largely the result of an increasing orientation towards the literature, manners and mood of the 18th century, especially those of France. At the end of 1895 this led him to begin drawing in a manner inspired by contemporary line engravings made after the paintings of the 18th-century French painter Watteau and other masters of the Rococo, a style characterized by the extensive use of small curved motifs and 'C'-scrolls.

With the advent of this new style, Beardsley's work took on a more settle and mature character. His compositions became more balanced, harmonious and essentially classical, and his technical powers as a draughtsman reached new heights. The sureness and control with which he executed such intricate drawings as *The Abbé*, one of his illustrations for *Under the Hill*, is particularly impressive. Most commentators also agree that this drawing is in many respects a fanciful self-portrait, and it serves to emphasize that Beardsley was a tremendous dandy, as indicated in a contemporary portrait by the French painter Jacques-Emile Blanche. Dandyism was a hallmark of many of the great Decadent poets and artists, including Baudelaire and Oscar Wilde, who summarized its significance in one of his epigrams: 'One should either wear a work of art or be a work of art'.

By dressing beautifully the Romantic artist can become a 'work of art', elevated from the utilitarian everyday world, as this passage from *Under the Hill* illustrates: 'The Abbé Franlefuche having lighted off his horse, stood doubtfully for a moment beneath the gateway of the mysterious Hill, troubed with an exquisite fear lest a day's travel should have undone the laboured niceness of his dress. His hand . . . played nervously about the gold hair that fell upon his shoulders like a finely curled peruke, and from point to point of a precise toilet the fingers wandered, quelling the little mutinies of cravate and ruffle.'

A number of other illustrations to *Under the Hill* display the same highly-wrought, fine, Rococo quality – *The Toilet* reworks one of Beardsley's perennial themes, and *The Ascension of Saint Rose of Lima* shows his fascination with the baroque elements of the Roman Catholic Church.

CHAPTER FOUR

POSTERS, BOOKCOVERS, THE RAPE OF THE LOCK & DAS RHEINGOLD

ONE IMPORTANT development in the applied arts in the 1890s was a boom in poster design. As in other areas, such as book printing, the catalyst was a technical development – in this case, lithography. The process of lithography was not new; it had been invented in 1798 by Alois Senefelder in Austria, although his methods were not fully perfected until later. By 1848 it was possible to print sheets at a rate of 10,000 per hour, and in 1866 the French designer Jules Cheret started to produce colour lithographic posters from his own press in Paris.

Cheret took the visual language of popular folk art, used to decorate circus programmes, and enlarged upon it. His posters bring together a traditional technique and an appreciation of great mural art, but more importantly, he also captured a feel for the popular idiom. Cheret's influence grew as young artists such as Henri de Toulouse-Lautrec, Pierre Bonnard and Alphonse Mucha found that the poster was a form of visual shorthand in which ideas could be expressed simply and directly. Poster artists managed to convey exactly the spirit of the era known as *fin de siècle* (end of the century), and also provided a decorative comment on the social life of the streets.

Paris was undoubtedly the centre of the development of poster art, and during his many trips to the French capital Beardsley must have seen work by Cheret and Lautrec plastered on every street corner.

In March 1894 Beardsley designed a striking blue and green poster for the play *A Comedy of Sighs* by John Todhunter, showing at the Avenue Theatre near Charing Cross station in London. The poster was among the earliest of its type and formed part of the first wave of Beardsley's art to attract public attention. *The Globe* described it as 'an ingenious piece of arrangement, attractive by its novelty and cleverly imagined. The mysterious female who looms through the transparent curtain is, however, unnecessarily repulsive in facial type'. That stodgy comment was echoed in a

RIGHT
Frontispiece for a satirical novel by John Davidson entitled *A Full Account of the Wonderful Mission of Earl Lavender*, which deals with Darwinian evolution and the religious practice of flagellation. The drawing shows how Beardsley's illustrative style was moving away from dense black masses towards the fine rococo linework characteristic of the 18th century.

AUBREY
BEARDSLEY

AVENUE THEATRE
(Licensed by the LORD CHAMBERLAIN to GEORGE PAGET, Esq.)
Northumberland Avenue, Charing Cross, W.C.
Manager - Mr. C. T. H. HELMSLEY
ON THURSDAY, March 29th, 1894,
And every Evening at 8-50,
A New and Original Comedy, in Four Acts, entitled,
A COMEDY OF SIGHS!
By JOHN TODHUNTER.
Sir Geoffrey Brandon, Bart. - Mr. BERNARD GOULD
Major Chillingworth - - Mr. YORKE STEPHENS
Rev. Horace Greenwell - - Mr. JAMES WELCH
Williams - - - - - - - Mr. LANGDON
Lady Brandon (Carmen) - - Miss FLORENCE FARR
Mrs. Chillingworth - - Miss VANE FEATHERSTON
Lucy Vernon - - - - - Miss ENID ERLE
Scene - THE DRAWING-ROOM AT SOUTHWOOD MANOR
Time—THE PRESENT DAY—Late August.
ACT I. - - - - AFTER BREAKFAST
ACT II. - - - - AFTER LUNCH
ACT III. - - - - BEFORE DINNER
ACT IV. - - - - AFTER DINNER
Preceded at Eight o'clock by
A New and Original Play, in One Act, entitled,
The LAND OF HEART'S DESIRE
By W. B. YEATS.
Mr. JAS. WELCH, Mr. A. E. W. MASON, & Mr. G. R. FOSS; Miss WINIFRED FRASER, Miss CHARLOTTE MORLAND, & Miss DOROTHY PAGET.
The DRESSES by NATHAN, CLAUDE, LIBERTY & Co., and BENJAMIN.
The SCENERY by W. T. HEMSLEY. The FURNITURE by HAMPDEN & SONS.
Stage Manager - - - - - Mr. G. R. FOSS
Doors open at 7-40, Commence at 8. Carriages at 11.
PRICES:--Private Boxes, £1 1s. to £4 4s. Stalls, 10s.6d.
Balcony Stalls, 7s. Dress Circle, 5s. Upper Circle (Reserved), 3s.
Pit, 2s.6d. Gallery, 1s.
On and after March 26th, the Box Office will be open Daily from 10 to 5 o'clock, and 8 till 10. Seats can be Booked by Letter, Telegram, or Telephone No. 35297.
NO FEES. NO FEES. NO FEES.

LEFT

Poster design for *A Comedy of Sighs*, among the earliest of its type. This was one of Beardsley's rare excursions into colour. The depiction of the female form provoked much criticism – a short satirical poem was dedicated to it ending 'Your Japanese Rossetti girl is not a thing to be desired.'

LEFT

Girl and a Bookshop, an excellent example of the art of harmonious dis-balance Beardsley had assimilated from his study of Japanese prints.

AVBREY
BEARDSLEY

lighter vein by the literary parodist, Owen Seaman, who dedicated a short satirical poem to Beardsley and the poster which concluded: 'Your Japanese Rossetti girl is not a thing to be desired'.

The design echoes the work of French poster artists, but again Beardsley modifies instead of merely imitating, to produce a unique piece of work. This was also one of his very few excursions into the use of colour, with a virulent lime green on a turquoise background.

LEFT

Invitation to the opening of Prince's Ladies Golf Club at Mitcham, Surrey. One of Beardsley's most splendid travesties of contemporary costume. The pierrot caddies are equally frivolous.

Beardsley was also commissioned to design a poster for *The Pseudonym and Antonym Libraries*, a series of cloth- and paper-bound books published by T Fisher Unwin. In this work, the drawing is focused on one side and towards the top – an excellent example of the art of 'harmonious dis-balance' Beardsley had assimilated from his study of Japanese prints. The design itself is based on an earlier line drawing, *Girl and a Bookshop*.

In another poster executed in 1894, this time for a series of children's books, Beardsley again challenged convention, with his ironical depiction of a young woman sitting in a winged grandfather chair. The intention may have been to represent a grandmother reading to her grandchildren from one of the books listed on the poster, but instead of age and maturity, Beardsley formulates a disturbing sensuality in the features of the woman. This was the kind of negligent irony which repelled many of his contemporaries and only served to further his notoriety.

An invitation Beardsley designed to the opening of a ladies' golf club in Surrey is in a similar tongue-in-cheek vein. Beardsley took the opportunity of making the ladies' dresses as unsuitable to golf as possible, and it constitutes one of his most splendid travesties of contemporary costume. If this was not enough, the lady golfers come complete with Pierrot-style caddies – further proof, if it were needed, that Beardsley lived in a world of his own. If normal people or institutions chose to employ him, then they suffered the consquences.

Beardsley's poster for Singer sewing machines shows a woman singing at a piano in the middle of a field. It is interesting to speculate as to how the man at Saatchi and Saatchi would react to the wholly redundant pun.

As seen, the generating force behind publisher John Dent's version of *Le Morte d'Arthur* was the desire to exploit the possibilities of cheap mass production, and thus reach a wider audience. But the aim was also to show that, contrary to the doctrines of the Arts & Crafts movement, a mass-produced object could still be a thing of beauty. The cover of *Le Morte d'Arthur* is an emphatic reminder that by the 1890s, a beautiful book cover did not neces-

sarily have to be the laborious product of a highly skilled craftsman.

The production of finely designed bookbindings, by stamping and printing a design on to cloth or board, had originally been pioneered by Dante Gabriel Rossetti and Whistler in the 1870s. It reached a peak in the 1890s, with contributions from many other besides Beardsley, notably Charles Ricketts and the English novelist Lawrence Houseman.

LEFT
A Caprice, one of only two surviving oil paintings by Beardsley. The atmosphere is similar to that of the Venetian artist Longhi. Although Beardsley had only a dormant colour sense, the handling of flesh shows promise and hints at future development.

One of Beardsley's most important book cover designs was for *The Houses of Sin* by Vincent O'Sullivan, an American-born writer whom Beardsley had come to know well in 1896. Beardsley thought that *The Houses of Sin* was 'quite O'Sullivan's best book,' and it inspired him to create a sumptuous and extraordinary design of a flying pig's head against an ornate baroque pillar. The use of the head was Beardsley's version of the traditional representation of the breeze as a winged head with puffed cheeks, but it also symbolizes the idea of sin embodied by the piggy-faced old harlot. The pillar which the 'breeze' is caressing is a portal of one of the 'houses of sin' described in the title poem of the collection, which also contains the image of the breeze as a seducer:

> 'Then, as a perfumed wind came glancing by,
> And kissed me with a melancholy sigh,
> And wooed me to its lair
> Of flower haunted rooms . . .'

The Houses of Sin is unusual because of its narrow, upright format, and also because the design was repeated on the back cover, apparently at the suggestion of that great connoisseur of beautiful books, Oscar Wilde. Beardsley also had very strong ideas about the cover design, namely that: 'it is to be printed in gold upon black smooth cloth. No other way. Purple, however, might be an alternative to print on.' In fact, the final choice as gold on cream.

THE BODLEY HEAD KEYNOTE SERIES: TOWARD THE 18TH-CENTURY LINE

In 1893, at around the time of the commission for *Salomé*, Beardsley also undertook to produce cover and title page designs for the Keynote series of novels published by Lane's company, The Bodley Head. The designs are excellent examples of what Joseph Pennell described in *The Studio* as Beardsley's ability to 'join extremes and reconcile what might be oppositions' in his

RIGHT
Design for the front cover for one of the *Keynote* series of novels

RIGHT
Scaramouche in Naxos, a good example of the bold and monumental effects Beardsley could achieve in his solid black and white compositions of *The Yellow Book* period.

use of the single line. Keynote was a series of 34 novels and volumes of short stories by young writers published by John Lane from 1893 onwards. They were produced relatively cheaply at 3s 6d, the aim being to make contemporary fiction available to a wide audience. For 22 of them Beardsley designed a cover which was also a title page, and for 15 he designed an orna-

mental key embodying the author's initials which was reproduced on the spine and back cover of the book. The title of the series, as well as a number of the individual titles such as *The Mirror of Music*, reflected the contemporary avant garde association of music with the other arts. Beardsley seems to have been particularly inspired by *The Mirror of Music*, since it is one of the most elaborate designs in the series. In the context of mass book production, Beardsley's involvement with the Keynote series was significant, since their cheapness brought about an increased circulation and awareness of good design.

ABOVE LEFT
Cover design for the bijou edition *The Rape of the Lock*.

ABOVE RIGHT
Cover design for the ordinary edition of *The Rape of the Lock*.

John Lane's publishing company also produced a range of prose, poetry and drama. Lane commissioned Beardsley to design several title page illustrations for these assorted works, among them a remarkable frontispiece for a volume of plays by John Davidson, a prominent minor poet, novelist and playwright of the 1890s. Like *The Wagnerites*, the illustration is an example of the bold and monumental effects Beardsley could achieve in his solid black and white compositions of *The Yellow Book* period. The drawing ostensibly relates to the final play in the volume, a pantomime called *Scaramouche in Naxos*, which Beardsley transforms into a vehicle for his own vision with a series of pantomime characters strategically deployed in a formal landscape. Each of the figures is probably a caricature portrait, of, among others, Mabel Beardsley, Oscar Wilde, Henry Harland (editor of *The Yellow Book*) and Beardsley himself.

In 1895, Beardsley completed another frontispiece for a book by John Davidson, a satirical novel, *A Full Account of the Wonderful Mission of Earl Lavender*, which deals with Darwinian evolution and the religious practice of flagellation. As usual, however, Beardsley's delicate drawing of a prim *flagellateuse* discharging her duty with amused hauteur, bears no resemblance to the relevant descriptive passage in the book. Executed in a precise, linear style, with no solid areas of tone, a comparison with the earlier frontispiece for Davidson's plays clearly shows the evolution Beardsley's technique was undergoing, away from the use of dense black masses and toward the fine rococo linework characteristic of the 18th century.

Some time in late 1895, the English poet and critic Edmund Gosse suggested to Beardsley that he should produce a set of illustrations for Alexander Pope's poem *The Rape of the Lock*. In view of his new 18th-century mood, it is perhaps not surprising that Beardsley seized the opportunity at once. The result was his third great illustrated book.

THE RAPE OF THE LOCK: A NEW RESPECT FOR THE TEXT

Pope's poem suited Beardsley perfectly – an elaborate satirical fantasy with an erotic theme, written in the severely classical style of heroic couplets, the form of epic poetry. It had originally been written in 1712, following an actual incident in which Lord Petre cut off a lock of hair from a Mrs Arabella Fermor, and precipated a bitter quarrel between their two families. Pope created a satirical masterpiece by dramatizing the events at length. The poem is dedicated to Arabella Fermor, and the signs are that Pope undertook the work to heal the breach between the two feuding families. How successful he was is unknown.

Both the lightheartedness and the classical feel of Pope's poem are reflected in Beardsley's illustrations, which are among the most restrained major drawings he ever made. Moreover, a new technical device is clearly apparent as Beardsley begins to use large quantities of dotted lines to create a rich stippled effect. But his emphasis on ornate embroideries and elaborate flounces of lace that he associated with the period led many critics at the

LEFT

The Baron's Prayer from *The Rape of the Lock*. Beardsley uses a 'pointilliste' drawing technique to create a rich stippled effect.

LEFT

A New Star. Footnote from *The Rape of the Lock*.

time to claim that Beardsley was nothing more than a supreme surface decorator. The illustrations go beyond being merely superficial fancies. In most of them the scenes are treated with great restraint as pictorial dramas – space is understood and implied, and in this respect the drawings are richer than those made for Salomé. Indeed, the black fields and arabesque lines of the Salomé period are completely absent, and there are none of the traces of the curvilinear forms later adopted by the Art Nouveau artists.

This new illustrated version of *The Rape of the Lock* was published by Leonard Smithers in May 1896. Smithers was also the publisher of *The Savoy* magazine, and it was he who had stepped into the breach following the débâcle surrounding *The Yellow Book*. On the title page Smithers describes *The Rape of the Lock* as 'an heroi-comical poem in five cantos written by Alexander Pope, embroidered with nine drawings by Aubrey Beardsley'. The use of the word 'embroidered' was evidently meant to forestall complaints that Beardsley had not illustrated this famous work with sufficient accuracy, but in fact his drawings are much closer to the text than those for *Le Morte d'Arthur* and *Salomé*.

RIGHT
The Toilet from *The Rape of the Lock*. Beardsley depicts Belinda the heroine engaged in her toilet.

Four different editions of *The Rape of the Lock* were produced – an ordinary edition, a large paper edition and two *bijou* editions. By the late 1890s publishers regularly produced sumptuous 'large paper' editions of their books, usually distinguished from the ordinary editions by better quality paper and the use of real vellum instead of cloth for the binding. These various editions of *The Rape of the Lock* which Smithers saw fit to produce give a good idea of the increased market for beautiful and expensive editions in the 1890s. The two cover designs which Beardsley produced – one for the ordinary editions and one for the pocket-sized *bijou* editions are both examples of rococo exuberance, entirely in keeping with the spirit of the book.

At the start of the poem, Pope introduces the heroine Belinda, whose character was based, with some artistic licence, on Mrs Arabella Fermor:

> 'This Nymph to the Destruction of Mankind
> Nourish'd two Locks which graceful hung behind
> In equal curls, and well conspir'd to deck
> With shining Ringlets the smooth Ivr'y Neck.
> Love in these Labyrinths his Slaves detains,
> And mighty Hearts are held in slender Chains.'

In the first full page illustration, *The Toilet*, Beardsley pictures Belinda at her toilet. Graded dots are used in a 'pointillist' effect to suggest varied tones in the *trompe l'oeil* landscape decoration on a screen, on the elaborate lace flounces of the women's clothes, and for the vertical patterns on the wallpaper. The contrasting textures and tone realize to perfection one of the most captivating passages in the poem, and one which Beardsley clearly relished.

The second illustration, *Le Billet Doux*, was reproduced as a headpiece on the first page of the opening canto. Belinda, seen in her boudoir reading a love letter, is endowed with an absurd, almost cloying prettiness. More importantly, however, the style of this illustration appears to move away from the disintegrative compositions of Beardsley's previous drawings, which were heavily influenced by the 'dis-balanced harmony' of Japanese art. Here, the figure is only slightly off centre, and is counter-balanced by details such as the nearly symmetrical bedhead and the wallpaper above. *The Rape of the Lock* thus marked a turning point in Beardsley's compositional development, with balanced, centralized compositions becoming more frequent.

LEFT
The Rape of the Lock. Beardsley depicts the Baron poised over Belinda's head, about to cut off a lock of her hair. The setting is a lavish party at a fashionable country house.

This is also clear in the fourth illustration, *The Baron's Prayer*, which places the figure of the Baron at the centre of the drawing. The Baron has been captivated by Belinda's locks of hair, and Beardsley shows him praying at a makeshift altar to love, constructed of French erotic novels and bits of his previous mistresses' underwear, on which he lights a sacrificial fire of old love letters. Pope describes the scene in the following passage:

'. . . to Love an Altar built
Of twelve vast French Romances, neatly gilt.
There lay three Garters, half a Pair of Gloves,
And all the Trophies of his former Loves.
With tender Billet-doux he lights the Pyre,
And breathes three am'rous sighs to raise the Fire.
Then prostrate falls, and begs with ardent Eyes
Soon to obtain and long possess the Prize.'

The Prize is, of course, a lock of Belinda's hair, and the Baron's prayer is eventually answered. In the sixth illustration, entitled *The Rape of the Lock*, Beardsley captures the moment of suspense before the Baron furtively wields his scissors in Belinda's direction:

'The Peer now spreads his glittering Forfex wide,
T'inclose the Lock; now joins it to divide.
The meeting Points the sacred Hair dissever
From the fair Head, for ever and for ever!'

The setting for the action is a fashionable coffee party, held in the grandeur of a country house. The central feature of the composition is a sagacious-looking dwarf, an ironic touch which was

characteristic of much of Beardsley's work. The remaining elements in the picture are successfully balanced behind the dwarf – the elaborate clothes of the fellow revellers, the stippled curtains, the picture window and the landscaped park beyond. The women's clothes are not an accurate reflection of early 18th-century fashions, but they suit the playful hauteur, the amusement at pretension and folly that are at the heart of the poem.

On realizing what the Baron has done to her precious coiffeur, Belinda is naturally incensed. This gives Pope the opportunity to concoct a long and fanciful account of the domain of the goddess of Spleen, or ill temper, where Umbriel, a dusky melancholy sprite goes to seek further fuel for Belinda's wrath. This passage is the most fantastic and grotesque in the poem, and evidently appealed to Beardsley, who produced a bizarre composition populated with the strange creatures described by Pope. To the right of the drawing is the goddess of Spleen herself:

LEFT
The Battle of the Beaux and the Belles from *The Rape of the Lock*. This drawing is an incomparable image of a beautiful woman in a rage with a man. The Baron kneels before Belinda in mock supplication and begs forgiveness for his crime. The wealth of detail is astonishing.

'And screen'd in Shades from Day's detested Glare,
She sighs forever on her pensive Bed,
Pain at her Side, and Megrim at her Head.'

Behind her is:

'. . . Ill-nature like an ancient Maid,
Her wrinkled form in Black and White array'd . . .'

As for the rest:

'Unnumber'd Throngs, on ev'ry side are seen,
Of bodies chang'd to various forms by Spleen.
Here living Teapots stand, one Arm held out . . .'

At the centre of this fantastic composition Beardsley added the figure of Alexander Pope, clad in a spotted robe and cap, staring out from this exotic and sinister tableau.

Duly encouraged by the gift from the goddess of Spleen, Belinda eventually confronts the Baron and demands the return of her hair. He refuses. Belinda then resorts to force, and defeats the Baron by throwing snuff in his face:

'See fierce Belinda on the Baron flies,
With more than usual Lightening in her Eyes:
Just where the Breath of Life his Nostrils drew,
A charge of Snuff the wily Virgin threw;'

In *The Battle of the Beaux and the Belles*, Beardsley shows the Baron defeated, kneeling before Belinda, and prepared, in a mock heroic manner to die, except:

'All that I dread, is leaving you behind!
Rather than so, ah! let me still survive,
And burn in Cupid's Flames – but burn alive.'

LEFT
The Cave of Spleen from *The Rape of the Lock*. Right at the centre of this strange assortment of fantastic forms is a caricature of the poem's author, Alexander Pope.

This is another of Beardsley's masterpieces. Absolutely classical in composition, it is balanced, harmonious and monumental, yet at the same time vividly expressive of the emotions of the two protagonists. The fallen rococo chair, completely natural in the circumstances, is a brilliant compositional device for blocking the foreground and creating a sense of real space for the figures behind. Among a profusion of individual details, the rendering of the Baron's brocade coat is particularly breathtaking.

The poem concludes with the following admonition to Belinda, which suggests that although she may have lost a lock of hair, the incident has conferred upon her a kind of immortality:

'When those fair Suns shall set, as set they must,
And all those Tresses shall be laid to dust;
This Lock, the Muse shall consecrate to fame,
And 'midst the stars inscribe Belinda's Name!'

'THE LEAST REPOSEFUL, MOST TROUBLED AND CONFUSING THING'

The ten drawings for *The Rape of the Lock* were begun in London in early January 1896 and completed two months later in Paris, where Beardsley had been living since the beginning of February. 'Paris suits me very well,' he wrote to Smithers, 'I don't know when I shall return to London – filthy hole – where I get nothing but snubs and the cold shoulder.'

Around the middle of March, however, he decided to go to Brussels with Smithers. There the tuberculosis suddenly reasserted itself. He suffered a haemorrhage of the lung, and was forced to remain in Brussels until early May, when he was then considered well enough to be brought back to London.

During the remaining months of his life, Beardsley embarked upon a number of projects, most of which were to remain unfinished. One of these was a set of drawings illustrating *The Comedy of the Rhinegold*, which was based on Wagner's famous opera *Das Rheingold*.

RIGHT
The Third Tableau of *Das Rheingold*, one of an unfinished series of illustrations depicting the legend which forms the basis of the famous Wagnerian opera *Das Rheingold*.

RIGHT
Illustration for the Fourth Tableau of *Das Rheingold*.

Beardsley completed five drawings and a frontispiece, all of which were published separately in various editions of *The Savoy* magazine. The most notable illustrations in the series are those of the Third and Fourth Tableaux. In *The Third Tableau*, Wotan, King of the Gods and Loge, the God of Fire, are in the underworld, attempting to recover the magical gold stolen by the dwarf Alberich, who was metamorphosed into a huge coiled serpent. In *The Fourth Tableau*, which formed the cover of *The Savoy* No.6, Loge and Wotan have triumphed over Alberich and forced him to return the gold. Beardsley pictures them on the mountains where the gods dwell, pointing triumphantly down at the recovered

treasure. This is one of the most boldly dis-balanced of all Beardsley's compositions, and the flame-shaped robes and hair of the fire god are unique visual inventions.

The Third Tableau was published as an illustration to the second part of *Under the Hill* in *The Savoy* No.2 in April 1896. *Das Rheingold* appears in *Under the Hill* as one of the Abbé Fanfeluche's bedside books, and there is an appreciative description of it which clearly appealed strongly to Beardsley:

'... Alberich's savage activity and metamorphosing, and Loge's rapid, flaming tongue-like movements, make the tableau the least reposeful, most troubled and confusing thing in the whole range of opera. How the Abbé rejoiced in the extravagant monstrous poetry, the heated melodrama and splendid agitation of it all!'

CHAPTER FIVE
THE FINAL SERIES, LYSISTRATA, BEARDSLEY'S DEATH

RIGHT
Drawing for the frontispiece of *Lysistrata*, the erotic comedy by Aristophanes.

The attack of tuberculosis suffered by Beardsley while visiting Paris in March 1896 marked the beginning of the end. The last 22 months of his life were spent constantly on the move in search of health, and constantly battling to produce as much work as possible before the disease finally claimed his life. When he returned to London in the early summer of 1896 he consulted a specialist, Dr Symes Thompson, and learnt that he was seriously ill – 'I am beginning to be really depressed and frightened about myself,' he wrote in a letter at this time. In July 1896 he made his will, but for some time he held his ground, and throughout 1896 produced work of astonishing quality at a feverish pace.

Immediately after *The Rape of the Lock* had been completed, Leonard Smithers commissioned Beardsley to illustrate a translation he planned to publish of the Greek erotic comedy *Lysistrata* by Aristophanes. Beardsley completed this commission, for eight large drawings, between late June and early August 1896 while staying at The Spread Eagle hotel in Epsom. The book was published 'privately' by Smithers later in the year, in a limited edition of 100 copies. *Lysistrata* was Beardsley's fourth, and, as it turned out, his last great illustrated work. The quartet of masterpieces are all the more astonishing for being so different from one another, and form the four cornerstones of Beardsley's art.

Aristophanes (445 BC–386 BC) was the most celebrated comic poet of ancient Athens. *Lysistrata* was written and first performed in Athens in 411 BC at the height of a series of devastatingly destructive wars between the city states of Athens and Sparta (also known as Lacedaemon). The theme of the play concerns the attempt by the Athenian and Spartan women, led by the remarkably modern Lysistrata, to end the war by withdrawing sexual favours from the men until they agree to stop fighting. Aristophanes obtains a great deal of very bawdy and extremely funny mileage out of the mens' plight, but the play's underlying message of the waste and futility of war is deeply serious.

LYSISTRATA.
AUBREY BEARDSLEY.

AUBREY BEARDSLEY.

In *Two Athenian Women in Distress*, Beardsley pictures one woman descending on the rope, and renders quite literally, the image of the other attempting to escape on the back of a sparrow, with Lysistrata's arm reaching for her hair from outside the top edge of the drawing, in a striking piece of composition.

In one of the most elegant drawings of the series, *Cinesias Entreating Myrrhina to Coition*, Beardsley visualizes the scene in which Cinesias, husband of Myrrhina, returns from the fighting in an extremely 'deprived' state – as Lysistrata puts it – '. . . writhing in Aphrodite's love grip'. She instructs Myrrhina to tease him until he is in such a state that he will agree to anything, even peace with Sparta. The result is one of the most brilliantly sustained comic scenes in the history of the theatre, ending with Cinesias completely bewildered and still unsatisfied. Beardsley accurately envisages his frustrated condition as he fruitlessly pursues his wife around the stage.

LEFT
Lysistrata Haranguing the Athenian Women. In this illustration, Lysistrata is attempting to persuade the women of Athens to withhold their favours from their husbands in order to stop the war with neighbouring Sparta.

The full impact of the women's strike is soon made clear by the arrival of a herald from Sparta, followed by a group of ambassadors come to sue for peace. All are in the same painful condition. Beardsley records this scene in *The Lacedaemonian Ambassadors*, a drawing which has both startling and absurd qualities. The tallest and youngest ambassador has a piled head of hair, which recalls the hermaphrodite figure in *The Mirror of Love* and many of the young men in *Le Morte d'Arthur*. The phalluses are abnormally large to symbolize anticipation and frustration, and the manner in which this gross indecency is combined with classical simplicity is equal to the rumbustious nature of Aristophanes' text.

Following this encounter with the ambassadors, Lysistrata makes a speech of masterly diplomacy and finally succeeds in bringing the warring factions to terms.

As soon as he had finished *Lysistrata* Beardsley turned his attention to classical Rome, and began illustrating *The Sixth Satire* of the Latin poet Juvenal. *The Sixth Satire* was intended to be a savage denunciation of the morals of upper-class Roman women of Juvenal's period (c. AD 55–138). Singled out for particular attention was Messalina, the depraved and murderous wife of the Emperor Claudius. Her capacity for avarice, lust and cruelty was legendary and eventually Claudius was forced to have her executed.

In one passage Juvenal describes her habit of leaving the Imperial Palace every night to become a whore in a brothel, and this inspired Beardsley to make two drawings of Messalina which must rank among his most explicit studies in evil.

LEFT
One of the most elegant drawings in this series is *Cinesias Entreating Myrrhina to Coition.* All the Lysistrata drawings reflect something of the Greek vase spirit, which Beardsley had studied at the British Museum.

LEFT
The Lacedaemonian Ambassadors – the oversize phalluses which are intended to symbolise sexual frustration give this drawing its startling and absurd qualities.

The first, completed in 1895 and entitled simply *Messalina*, clearly relates to the night pieces of his Yellow Book period; indeed, the suggestion is much more of 1890s London than of ancient Rome. However in every other way the image closely corresponds to Juvenal's description of the depraved Messalina: '. . . that whore empress – who dared to prefer the mattress of a stews to her couch in the Palace, called for her hooded night cloak and hastened forth, alone, or with a single maid to attend to her. Then, her black hair hidden under an ash-blonde wig, she would make straight for the brothel . . .'

Beardsley conveys a powerful sense of what some might

define as evil, others as an unslaked perversion or misdirection of erotic energy, not only in Messalina's head, but also in all her accoutrements – her shoe, her dress and the twisted corner of her cloak. Everything is achieved by solid areas of black and white, including the brutal lurch forward of Messalina's body.

A year later, Beardsley produced another drawing of the depraved empress, this time returning from a night of debauchery described by Juvenal in the following passage:

'Retiring exhausted, yet still far from satisfied, cheeks begrimed with lamp smoke, filthy, carrying home, to her imperial couch the stink of the whorehouse'.

Beardsley depicts her dishevelled return, her fists clenched in continuing frustration. This drawing is in the style of the *Lysistrata* series, the impact being achieved by the use of a thick, sensuous line to convey Messalina's gross power. The purposeful pose of the female figure is surmounted by one of the most plain frightening of Beardsley's heads and yet it is still recognizable as a corrupted variant of his ideal woman, and in this lies its extraordinary power to affect the viewer. Does the drawing display, as has been widely supposed, a hatred of women; a disdain for the evil of corruption? Even to argue that the image is a *celebration* of corruption, the attitude to Beardsley's work which characterized so many of his contemporaries, cannot be dismissed.

LEFT
This illustration of the Roman empress Messalina is widely regarded as one of Beardsley's most explicit studies in evil. Here she is seen departing for a night of lust in a brothel. The solid black and white masses lend force to the perverted power of the so-called 'whore empress'.

RIGHT
Self-portrait by Beardsley. The coat is Regency in cut, the frilled shirt an imaginary garment.

RETURNING TO A FINER LINE

Towards the end of 1896 Beardsley returned to his former fine line rococo style of drawing, with a set of illustrations for *The Pierrot of the Minute*, a play by Ernest Dowson, an English poet of the Decadent school. Beardsley had previously produced a cover for a collection of Dowson's verses, which was a masterpiece of Art Nouveau design at its most elegantly simple. For *The Pierrot of the Minute* Beardsley was able to use the pantomime figure of the Pierrot, the clown, a familiar image which occurred frequently throughout his work. Pierrots also played an important part in the iconography of the 1890s, and survived into the work of artists such as Picasso and the French engraver Georges Rouault.

No doubt Beardsley's Pierrot images involved a certain amount of self-identification – in an illustration for Molière's play *Don Juan*, published in *The Savoy* No. 6, the central figure of Don Juan is based on Beardsley's idealized image of himself.

The Pierrot of the Minute was described by its author as 'a dramatic phantasy in one act' and was published by Leonard Smithers in March 1987. The covers of the edition of 300 copies

ABOVE
Front cover design for *The Pierrot of the Minute*, Beardsley's last completed commission.

RIGHT
Illustration for *The Pierrot of the Minute*. The dense vegetation is reminiscent of the French painter Watteau.

were bound in green cloth: those of the deluxe edition were bound in Japanese vellum. A design of a Pierrot holding an hour glass to symbolize the passage of time was stamped in gold on the front covers of both editions.

Two of the illustrations are of a particularly haunting beauty – those for the frontispiece and the *cul-de-lampe* (tailpiece). Both depict the figure of Pierrot in a garden with trellises, lilies, stylized roses and tall trees, which purports to be the garden of the Palace of Versailles. The dense rendering of the vegetation is reminiscent of the 18th-century French artist Watteau, who also used Pierrot imagery in his paintings. The drawing for the *cul-de-lampe* reveals yet again Beardsley's gift for design, in the white disbalanced figure of Pierrot moving out of the picture. His head, divided by a bald line from his hat, might be said to be derived from one of Watteau's Pierrots, but the embittered expression is Beardsley's comment on the character of Pierrot in what he calls a 'foolish playlet'.

The Pierrot of the Minute was Beardsley's last completed commission. By the time it was published in March 1897, the tuberculosis had advanced to the point where it prevented him from working for long stretches at a time. In April 1897 he spent some time in Boscombe, Bournemouth, reduced to a state of great weakness. Intimations of mortality continued to preoccupy him, and he had been formally converted to the Roman Catholic Church some months earlier.

On the advice of his doctors he continued to travel, visiting Dieppe and the south of France. In the autumn of 1897 he was back in Paris, but medical advice was not in favour of him risking another winter in that city. Thus in November, Beardsley and his mother, who had been with him for most of the time since Bournemouth, set off for Menton in the south of France, on the French/Italian border. There, in the confines of The Hotel Cosmopolitan, he remained bedridden, but still working whenever possible. He seldom gave up working, unless incapacitated by the chills and haemorrhages that ravaged him, and his feverish productivity when active was linked indirectly to the fever generated in him by the tuberculosis.

A photograph taken in early 1898 shows him seated in his room at The Hotel Cosmopolitan, alert and soigné as ever. The walls are covered with reproductions of Mantegna's engravings and in front of them hangs a symbolic crucifix. He died during the night of March 15, having received the last sacraments, and was buried in the cemetery at Menton overlooking the old town. He was 25.

A.B.

On hearing of Beardsley's demise Oscar Wilde wrote to Smithers with his characteristic generosity: 'I am greatly shocked to read of poor Aubrey's death. Superbly premature as the flowering of his genius was, he still had immense powers of development and had not sounded his last stop. There were great possibilities always in the cavern of his soul.'

Although Beardsley produced relatively little during the last 15 months of his life, he was full of plans. He had begun an ambitious scheme of illustrations for Ben Jonson's play *Volpone,* and a smaller group of drawings for Theophile Gautier's romantic novel *Mademoiselle de Maupin.* Both sets of illustrations remained incomplete at his death, but they hinted at great things to come and show that his creative powers remained undiminished.

LEFT
D'Albert in Search of His Ideals from *Mademoiselle de Maupin* by Theophile Gautier. Beardsley's leaning toward caricature has become noticeably more exaggerated in this illustration.

'ANY NUMBER OF PRAYERS'

In the illustrations to *Mademoiselle de Maupin*, eventually published by Leonard Smithers in 1898, there are signs that Beardsley was developing a new style. He dropped his severely black and white technique for one consisting of line and wash, and the resulting intermediate tones had to be reproduced by photogravure as opposed to lineblock. It showed him as a master of tone grading as well as tone contrasts, and the same neatness, precision and uncompromisingly definitive exposition of ideas can be seen in terms of this new technique. His growing sense and awareness of three dimensions, which formerly he had merely implied, he now wished to exploit more fully.

In *The Lady at the Dressing Table* from *Mademoiselle de Maupin*, his constant preoccupation with toilet scenes is expressed all the more vividly by his play on vanishing points, a primitive feat on similar lines to the jagged, distortive exploits of early Cubist painters such as Picasso and Braque.

Mademoiselle de Maupin itself was written by the French novelist and poet Theophile Gautier at the age of 24, and was first published in 1835. It is a hymn to erotic love and the love of visual beauty as the cardinal elements in life. It is the source of the doctrine 'art for art's sake' and thus became a key text for the whole of the Romantic and Decadent movement in art and literature.

When Beardsley was commissioned to illustrate it, he must have been aware that he was living on borrowed time. In a letter to a friend dated August 1897 he wrote: '*Mademoiselle de Maupin* is the book and is to be printed in French and eight monthly parts. You may offer up any number of prayers for the completion of the pictures.'

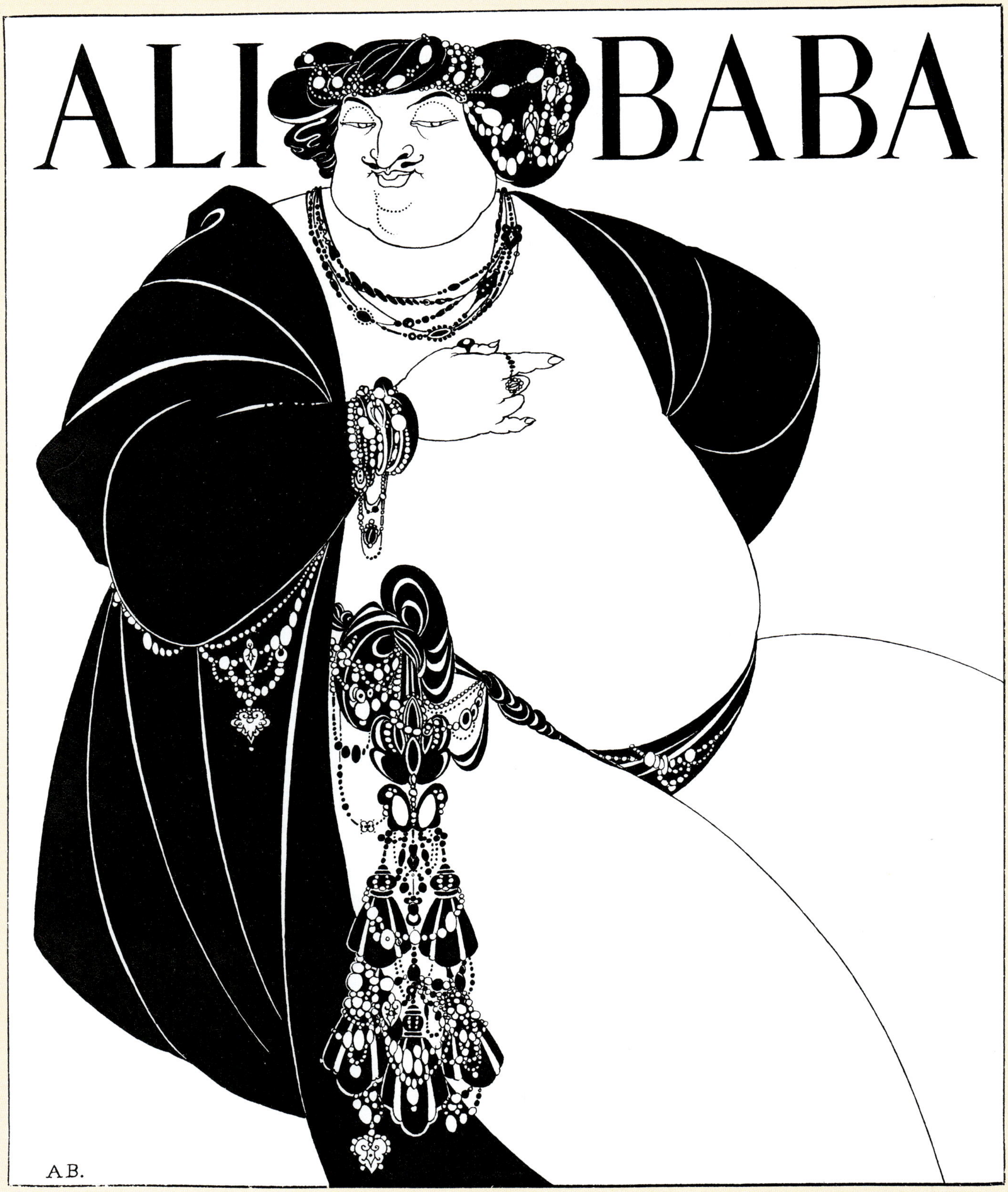
ALI BABA
A.B.

At the core of the book is the story of a triangular love affair between D'Albert, the young poet hero, his mistress Rosette, and the outrageously handsome Theodore, who in reality is a woman, Mademoiselle de Maupin. In an illustration entitled *The Lady with the Monkey*, Beardsley captures the moment in the book when Maupin appears as a woman for the first time, described by Gautier in the following passage:

'A sharp ray of light illumined her from head to foot . . . she sparkled as if the light were emanating from her instead of simply being reflected, and you would have taken her for a wonderful creature of the brush rather than a human being made from flesh and blood.'

LEFT
Ali Baba. Drawing intended for a proposed version of *The Forty Thieves*, which was never undertaken. It manages to combine the dramatic contrast between black and white forms with the tense detail of *The Rape of the Lock* series.

Beardsley's Maupin is indeed a 'wonderful creature of the brush', and one of the greatest examples in art of imagined female beauty. It is particularly remarkable for its delicate but powerful sensuality, achieved by the use of graded areas of tone, richly embellished with rococo linework. The monkey on the window ledge acting as master of ceremonies is Beardsley's own invention and further proof of his extraordinary draughting skill.

'AVE ATQUE VALE'

The final series of drawings Beardsley undertook was for Ben Jonson's play *Volpone*, or *The Red Fox*. which was first performed in 1607. Leonard Smithers commissioned Beardsley towards the end of 1897, but by his death in March 1898, Beardsley had completed only the cover, the frontispiece and a series of small drawings illustrating letters of the alphabet. Smithers published two editions of *Volpone* – an ordinary edition with a cover design of gold stamped on turquoise cloth, and a large paper edition with a cover stamped on vellum. Beardsley produced the design for the cover while staying at the Hotel Foyot in Paris in November 1897. It was originally intended as the cover for a series of drawings illustrating the story of Ali Baba, but in his desperation to complete *Volpone* in the last months of his life, Beardsley transferred it.

The last of his great drawings is the frontispiece which shows Volpone gloating over his fraudulently obtained treasure, described in the opening lines of the play:

> 'Good morning to the day; and next, my gold;
> Open the shrine, that I may see my saint,
> Hail the world's soul and mine.'

A.B.

LEFT
The Lady with the Monkey from *Mademoiselle de Maupin*. This is the most elaborate example of Beardsley's ink wash technique which is used to achieve a range of intermediate grey tones.

LEFT
Ave Atque Vale. The title means 'Hail and Farewell', and can perhaps be regarded as the last explicit manifestation in Beardsley's art of his swiftly approaching death.

In style this drawing relates most closely to the illustrations for *The Rape of the Lock*, but the quality is more solid and weighty, and appropriately, in view of the play's date, is inspired by the manner of the 17th- rather than 18th-century engraving.

It also shows the great distance Beardsley had travelled from the medievalism of his very early works. The *Volpone* drawings reveal a concerted attempt to achieve two kinds of perfection. Firstly, that of a 17th-century line engraving, the reference and inspiration for the frontispiece reproduced in lineblock. Secondly,

A.B.

the baroque dramatization of light in order to realize his sense of the form of a particular object, which he introduced in the designs for the initial letters. These, like the drawings for *Mademoiselle de Maupin*, were reproduced in half-tone and photogravure.

One of the most successful was an illustration for the letter 'V', which shows the familiar image of an elephant with a basket of fruit (*howdah*) on its back. The drawing has a thick, ponderous force, and shows how Beardsley had abandoned his technique of merely suggesting outlines and silhouettes, in an attempt to dramatize the values of highlighting through the use of graded tones. He was also struggling to acquire a sculpturesque sense of feeling in the round – as if his approaching death brought an unconscious desire to assert the reality and solidity of his concepts.

LEFT
Illustration for the letter 'V' from *Volpone* by Ben Jonson. This shows Beardsley attempting to dramatize the values of highlighting through the use of gradual tones – a significant departure away from his familiar flat and simplified illustrative style.

Whether this intellectual approach could ever have been enriched by the sensuousness needed to bring such a technique to fruition, must remain one of the many unanswered questions surrounding Beardsley's remarkable art.

One drawing he made towards the end of his life makes a particularly poignant finale. *Ave Atque Vale* was reproduced in *The Savoy* magazine No. 7, November 1896. It is an illustration to the poem *Carmen CI* (Song 101) by the Latin poet Catullus, of which Beardsley made his own translation. The title means 'Hail and Farewell', which had a morbid relevance for Beardsley, then nearing the end of his own short life: the drawing and translation can perhaps be seen as the last explicit manifestation in his art of his awareness of approaching death.

By ways remote and distant waters sped,
Brother, to thy sad grave-side I am come,
That I may give the last gifts to the dead,
And vainly parley with thine ashes dumb:
Since she who now bestows and now denies
Hath ta'en thee, hapless brother, from mine eyes.

But lo! these gifts, these heirlooms of past years,
Are made sad things to grace thy coffin shell,
Take them, all drenched with a brother's tears,
And, brother, for all time, hail and farewell!

CHAPTER SIX

THE BEARDSLEY LEGACY . . . ART NOUVEAU AND THE SYMBOLISTS

RIGHT
The sinuous fleshy curves of the cover design for *Le Morte d'Arthur* epitomize the power and elegance of Art Nouveau design.

THE LEADING modern style at the turn of the century was Art Nouveau. Developed in the late 1880s, this movement in both the fine and applied arts was at its creative height in the subsequent decade. Art Nouveau originated partly in the English Arts & Crafts movement, but was adapted by individual countries throughout Europe and the United States. In each case, the interpretation of the style was linked with the idea of the 'new'; it represented new social developments, new technology and a new expression of the spirit. Although it encompassed the disciplines of architecture, glass, furniture, ceramics, and jewellery, it found its most complete expression through the graphic artist, and in this context, the work of Aubrey Beardsley is of particular significance.

The essence of Art Nouveau is line, a sinuous extended curve found in every design of this style. Art Nouveau artists rejected straight lines and right angles in favour of a more natural movement which pulsed with an organic vitality. These curving, flowing lines brought with them a feeling of lightness, grace and freedom.

Nature was the ultimate inspiration for Art Nouveau artists, particularly plants, insects and birds. Flowers, stems and leaves were chosen for their curving silhouettes, and most plant forms offered potential for development into an animated pattern. Beardsley's use of floral motifs in his illustrations for both *Le Morte d'Arthur* and *Salomé* exude the power and sensuality characteristic of Art Nouveau design. The fleshy, serpentine, over-ripe fleurs du mal which snake across the cover of *Le Morte d'Arthur* are a particularly fine example. These decorative values could also be applied to the curves of the female body and waves of flowing hair. Many of Beardsley's illustrations for *Le Morte d'Arthur* feature men and women with extravagantly curled locks – King Arthur is particularly *bouffant*, giving him a strange, hermaphroditic quality.

The influence of Japan was another key factor in the development of Art Nouveau. The 'harmonious disbalance' characteristic

of Japanese prints, which came flooding into Europe during the latter half of the 19th century, was an important feature of Beardsley's early work.

The main emphasis of Art Nouveau design was on decorative patterns and flatness – it was, in effect, a graphic style of decoration transposed on to a variety of solid objects, but it was at its most successful in a medium where line was the principal or only element. Book illustration, poster design and typography were all media in which the demands of mechanical reproduction limited the finer possibilities of tone and colour, the tools of the painter. Instead, graphic artists such as Beardsley concentrated their energies on strong designs and linear inventiveness. The best design was often that which acknowledged the inherent flatness of the medium and therefore concentrated on decorating the surface. This was part of a movement away from realism in the arts and towards fantasy and stylization of natural form, the generating forces behind Art Nouveau decoration.

THE EMERGENCE OF TYPOGRAPHY

Graphic artists aimed to combine visual images and the printed word to create a new form of illustration which was, in effect, a new strand of art. The idea was a harmonious integration of text and image, as opposed to isolated plates scattered throughout the volume. This fusion of different elements into a coherent

LEFT
The title page of Wren's City Churches *designed by Arthur Mackmurdo. This startling new use of free flowing lines was an early influence on British Art Nouveau designers, including Beardsley.*

RIGHT
John and Salomé. Beardsley's *Salomé* drawings collectively constitute a milestone in the development of Art Nouveau style. His extraordinary use of the whiplash curve has never been equalled.

overall design greater than the sum of its part was characteristic of Art Nouveau. The work of William Morris is a good example of this integrated approach. Morris designed new typefaces and used text and illustration as cohesive elements in the design of individual pages. But although Morris' work was of great significance, the medievally-inspired artists and designers of the English Arts & Crafts movement firmly resisted any temptation to adopt and develop the 'decadent' curvilinear style of Art Nouveau.

One of the first notable examples of lettering integrated with decoration was a title page illustration to *Wren's City Churches* by the English designer Arthur Mackmurdo in 1883. The sinuous, flame-like forms of the stylized flowers were reinterpreted by Beardsley more than ten years later in his designs for *The Comedy of the Rhinegold.*

RIGHT
Beardsley's bold style spanned a host of imitators – American illustrator Will Bradley was one of the more respectful. This design for a magazine faithfully copies Beardsley's technique, but the unsettling potency is definitely missing.

The first totally integrated publication in the Art Nouveau manner to be seen was *L'Histoire des Quatre Fils Aymon*, produced in 1883 by the French poster designer Eugène Grasset, who was to become one of the most influential Art Nouveau illustrators. Grasset, like Beardsley in *Le Morte d'Arthur*, chose a medieval legend, and spent over two years developing the decoration and illustration so that they became fused with the text. The actual style of the graphics was not fully-fledged Art Nouveau, but it was derived from the sources which inspired it – the Japanese emphasis on flat areas and outline, coupled with an intricate border decoration characteristic of Celtic illumination and carving.

Under the stern influence of William Morris, most artists and designers in England during the 1890s did not succumb to the curvilinear forms of this new and slightly suspect illustrative style. The exception was, of course, Beardsley, whose daring and sensuous refinement of Morris' stodgy medievalism provoked an acrimonious dispute between the two men. Morris was outraged by the result, which he regarded as running contrary to everything he was trying to encourage. But Beardsley, the great originator, was simply developing his own highly personal version of the Art Nouveau style.

He favoured asymmetry in the layout of the page, and natural detailing inspired by organic forms stylized into essentially artificial and very highly-refined decorative tableaux. Movement was generally conveyed through great, unbroken sinuous curves, and any sense of space or perspective was sacrificed in favour of a dramatic interplay between large simplified areas of pure black and white tone. Beardsley's sources were those of most Art Nouveau artists – medievalism, Japanese prints, an increasing

THE CHAP BOOK
THANKS GIVING NO.
WILL H BRADLEY

fascination with the 18th century, and a distinctive reinterpretation of early Renaissance decoration. Yet his work is startlingly original and of its time, deriving its impact from Beardsley's great knowledge of literature and art, coupled with the heightened sensibility of an invalid's delicate constitution.

THE ALLURE OF DECADENCE

Running parallel with the development of the tuberculosis was the development of his sexual imagination, also intensified by the ravages of disease. Beardsley was greatly attracted to sexual themes, and his work was peppered with graphic references to transvestism, hermaphroditism, flagellation, lesbianism, and other forms of sexual symbolism. This has often been interpreted as evidence of a homosexual inclination, coupled with the fact that he mixed with homosexual artists and writers, notably Oscar Wilde, in the literary and artistic circles of the 1890s. However, there is little reliable evidence to support this theory, and following the débâcle surrounding publication of *The Yellow Book*, Beardsley found it expedient to disassociate himself from the same circle of friends who had helped to further both his career and his notoriety. There is no doubt that his sexual imagination was highly developed, but in practice, if anything of a homosexual ideal occurred in Beardsley's life, it seems probable that it was cancelled by his sense of irony, thus contributing to the dramatic tension of his art.

Beardsley was fascinated by the decadence of his time, and perhaps his greatest works in the context of Art Nouveau are those for *Salomé*, in which he created a world of cruelly perverse sensuality, great visual refinement and exoticism, shot through with flashes of sardonic wit. It has the studied amorality of the *fin-de-siècle* dandy, as epitomized by both Beardsley and Oscar Wilde. Although Beardsley's sinister eroticism and distortions were very far removed from the freshness of most Art Nouveau flora and fauna, they were brought to life with the same asymmetrical elegance.

The character of Beardsley's world was unique, but his style attracted many imitators across Europe and the United States. The use of simple black and white with areas of rich embellishment set against areas of space was a technique that was essentially easy to copy, and imparted a strong impact with great economy. Since Beardsley's designs were largely in book or magazine format, they were easily transportable, and thus ended up being widely circulated in large numbers. This was particularly true of his illustrations for *The Yellow Book* and *The Savoy*.

RIGHT
An early Symbolist painting entitled *Vision after the Sermon* by the French artist Paul Gauguin. The Symbolist movement sought to reject naturalistic representation and express moods, ideas and emotion by flat planes of brilliant colour separated by thick black lines.

Many of Beardsley's imitators were extremely derivative, but there is clear evidence that his style, if used intelligently, formed part of a broader synthesis of Art Nouveau design. In the United States, the work of illustrator Will Bradley owed a very strong debt to Beardsley. Bradley worked in Chicago and was self-taught, without first hand exposure to European influence. Like most American designers of the time, he originally based his style on the Arts & Crafts movement, but became increasingly drawn towards Beardsley's early illustrations for *Le Morte d'Arthur*. Bradley employed the fluid lines of Art Nouveau to separate the black and white masses of Beardsley, but he retained a freshness and innocence which Beardsley singularly lacked.

English commentator F Scotson-Clark, who visited America during the 1890s, remarked: 'During the latter half of 1893 and the early half of 1894, the name of Aubrey Beardsley has become known, and popular as his success was among a large class in England, his fame was tenfold in America. Every town had its Beardsley artist, and large cities were simply teeming with them. Some borrowed his ideas and adapted them to their own use; others imitated them, until one asked oneself, "Is this done by the English or American B?".'

The 'American B' was Bradley, who eventually became sufficiently successful to publish his own occasional magazine, emphatically entitled *Bradley – His Book.*

A more refined interpretation of Beardsley's style is to be found in the elegantly and fully dressed ladies of Georges de

Feure's graphic works. De Feure was a Dutch artist whose proclivity for bizarre dwarfish grotesques and exaggerated costume details, best seen in his illustrations for Marcel Schwab's *La Porte des Rêves*, reveal a strong debt to Beardsley. His work has a startling animated vitality, which also recalls that of the French poster artist Jules Cheret, whom he originally trained under.

De Feure's interior designs represent a refined form of Art Nouveau, moving towards the classic simplicity of the 18th century, always richly adorned, but with a degree of restraint. Like Beardsley, de Feure was more concerned with book and magazine illustrations than commercial advertising. His posters feature galleries and exhibitions associated with his own Art Nouveau style. The de Feure female depicted in these works is generally a fur-coated, hatted, literary and artistic lady, closely related to her English cousin in the work of Beardsley.

RIGHT
A Musician by French artist Eugène Grasset. Many Symbolist paintings tended to resemble posters with their subjective colour and striking imagery.

THE SYMBOLISTS

De Feure was also involved with the Symbolist movement, which originated in France in 1889 when Paul Gauguin and other artists exhibited their work as 'Synthetist' painters. The object of the movement was the expression of ideas, moods, and emotion, coupled with a complete rejection of naturalistic representation. Their pictures were painted in brilliant colours separated by black lines, which sought to be both decorative and abstractive. Symbolist artists used the writhing linear patterns and amorphous shapes of Art Nouveau to describe things both sacred and profane, images which could express passion and excitement, but at the same time were loaded with classical, literary or religious references. Salomé, the Sphinx, Pan, Medusa, child-women and the serpent are all subjects of Symbolist painting, posters and poetry – for the movement was a fusion of parallel literary as well as artistic developments.

The pictorial designs of the artists connected with this movement directly affected graphic art such as book illustrations and posters, since they did not have to be presented in a naturalistic way. Enlarged decorative borders composed of eyes and ancient signs are mixed together with little regard for the traditional rules of pictorial composition. Many Symbolist paintings look like posters, with their allegorical subject matter, subjective colour and striking imagery. This revival of iconography was of great importance to both painting and graphics. The use of symbols in a design gives that work its own reality; objects do not need to be arranged within the naturalistic constraints of a single viewpoint hitherto imposed by traditional painting.

Perhaps the most impressive example of commercial symbolism, showing how an advertisement could make use of these developments, is the poster *Delftsche Slaolie,* designed in 1895 by the Dutch artist Jan Toorop. This work contains a synthesis of Art Nouveau devices and stylization (as well as a bottle of salad oil): Toorop uses the flowing hair of the two female figures to fill every available area of space, so the whole becomes a mass of hypnotically undulating rhythms. Toorop was also interested in the work of Morris and Beardsley, and this is reflected in his blending of fashionable eroticism and the occult, and his distorted elongated forms derived from the shadow puppets of Java.

Towards the end of the 19th century, the style of Art Nouveau was developed within individual countries into distinctive movements, each with their own distinct groups of designers and writers. The Glasgow School was the Scottish contribution to this new development, and was the result of several overlapping trends – the Arts & Crafts movement and its striving for renewal; the pre-Raphaelite school; Symbolism with its literary and artistic tendencies; the refined art of Japan; and the Celtic revival, with its strong nationalistic urge. With the appearance on the contemporary scene of an artist of the stature of Charles Rennie Mackintosh, Scottish Art Nouveau gained a figurehead who seized upon the cultural fragments of the age, giving them independent form. Mackintosh and his contemporaries helped to mould and develop the Glasgow School, which again owed a distinct stylistic debt to Beardsley.

Mackintosh was originally working as an architect in 1889. Two others in the group were the sisters Margaret and Frances MacDonald, the first of whom married Mackintosh, while the other married Herbert MacNair, the fourth member of the group. Between 1893 and 1894, 'The Glasgow Four', as they eventually became known, were engaged in producing a series of linear drawings and posters. They eagerly devoured *The Studio* magazine, which at that time contained Beardsley's illustrations for *Salomé*, and a painting by Jan Toorop entitled *The Three Brides*. The elegance of line, balance of dark and light and the infusion of Symbolism clearly had a major effect on The Four. What did not influence them, however, was Beardsley's predilection for malevolence, underscored with sexual symbolism.

This is not to suggest that the drawings, decorative panels and posters produced by The Four from 1893 onwards were in any sense great art. Much of the work was ephemeral in the extreme, and much of it was reducible to a simple formula which was repeated with varying degrees of success – rigid, rectilinear organization with extreme vertical emphasis, stylized animal and vegetable forms, and colour used only as a muted accent. But it did have an inward consistency which entitles it to the distinction of a style, and in the case of Mackintosh, it led to significant developments during the early 20th century. Many of Beardsley's drawings contained architectural settings with a sense of space which was to influence Mackintosh, one of the founders of modern architecture.

Just as the brief flowering of Art Nouveau had a profound effect on the development of modern design, so the short but productive life of Beardsley had a far-reaching influence into the first half of the 20th century. It was largely Beardsley's style, rather than his subject matter which accounted for this effect on pioneers of modern art such as Edvard Munch, Paul Klee and even the young Picasso, who in an early line drawing illustrates a scene from *Salomé*, inspired by Beardsley's designs for the same play.

In the final analysis it is hard to classify Beardsley. His art was new at the time of its making, and it is still new today – he alone has created the taste by which he is to be judged or enjoyed. His followers or imitators never really grasped his essential quality – the cold, clear, biting line, unmatched in European art, the perfection of balance in his designs, his daring use of black and

RIGHT
Menacing Head by Paul Klee. Beardsley's influence can be traced to several pioneers of modern art.

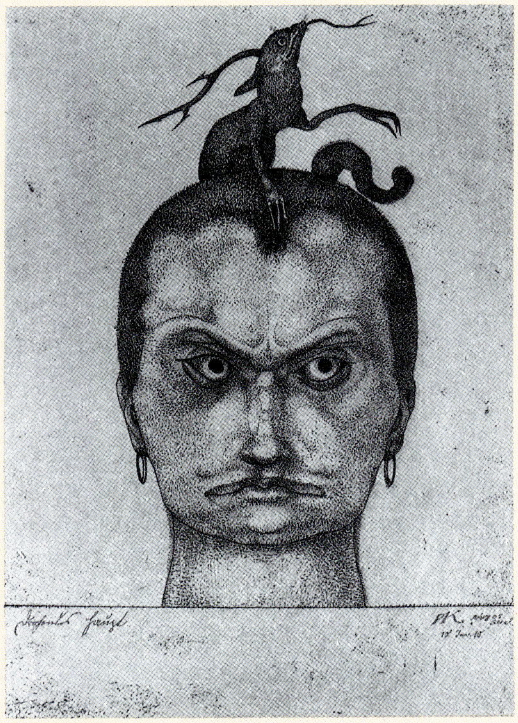

ABOVE
A Nocturne of Chopin intended for the ill-fated fifth volume of *The Yellow Book.* Beardsley employs washes to create a subtle range of tones, rather than the pure black and white he habitually used. It also shows the continuing influence of Whistler.

white and white masses and his unerring instinct for the correct values. His best drawings have a material excellence which paintings rarely have, like the sheer purity of a flawless stone.

That such rare and important qualities should be found together in one artist is highly unusual. But that they should be allied to great intelligence, ready wit, sardonic humour and dazzling powers of the imagination is a truly unique occurrence in the history of art.

INDEX

PICTURE CREDITS

Bridgeman Art Library pp 2, 14, 15, 17, 116, 123; Fogg Art Museum, Harvard University, Cambridge, Massachusetts, Bequest of Grenville L Winthrop pp 3, 13, 22, 30, 33, 40, 41, 42, 43, 44, 45, 60, 69, 73, 85, 106, 108, 112, 126 – Scofield Thayer Collection pp 64r, 84; Princeton University Library pp 7, 70, 76, 80, 82; *The Chap Book*, Chicago, August 1894 p 10; Tate Gallery pp 16, 53, 61, 78, 102; British Museum pp 18, 211, 48, 641; National Portrait Gallery p 25; The National Gallery, London p 26; Victoria and Albert Museum pp 21r, 27, 34, 35, 51, 52, 74, 75, 95, 101, 110, 119; The Drawing Shop, New York p 28; Mr F J Martin Dent p 29; The National Gallery of Canada p 37; Mary Evans Picture Library pp 47, 67, 97, 98, 111; The Metropolitan Museum of Art, Rogers Fund, 1952 pp 58; Royal Pavilion Art Gallery, Brighton p 63; Cleveland Museum of Art p 87; The Boston Museum of Fine Arts p 92; Museum of Art, Rhode Island School of Design p 94; Library of Congress, Rosenwald Collection p 104; Mr Brian Reade pp 115, 117; National Gallery of Scotland p 121; Kunst Museum, Berne p 125.
Every effort has been made to obtain copyright clearance for the illustrations in this book, and we apologise for any omissions.